THE GURUNGS OF NEPAL

Conflict and Change in a Village Society

Donald A. Messerschmidt

ARIS & PHILLIPS LTD., Warminster, England.

ISBN 0 85668 032 X (cloth)

ISBN 0 85668 050 8 (paper)

© Donald A. Messerschmidt, 1976. All rights reserved.
No part of this publication may be reproduced,
stored in a retrieval system, or transmitted,
in any form, or by any means without the prior
permission of the publishers.

Distributed in the USA and Canada by
ISBS, P. O. Box 555, Forest Grove, Oregon 97116, U.S.A.

Printed in England by Biddles Ltd., Guildford, Surrey

To Billi Ram, his friends, his neighbors

A Gurung Saying about Change:

kalo janchha, goro aunchha

Literally - 'the dark is replaced by the fair,'

or, ' . . . the old by the new.'

CONTENTS

PREFACE	x
A note on Foreign Terms and Quotations	xii
Acknowledgements	xiii
CHAPTER 1: THE GURUNGS OF NEPAL	1
Introduction	1
Gurung Social Organization	4
THE CHAR JAT CLANS	5
The Ghale	5
The Ghodane	5
The Lama	6
The Lamichane	6
THE SORA JAT	9
Tribal Hierarchy: The Basis of Social Conflict	9
Dual Hierarchy of the Jats	9
Four-fold Hierarchy and Lamichane Ascendancy	14
Lamichane Officials	17
CHAPTER 2: THE VILLAGE	24
Physical Setting	24
The Outside	27
Early Village History	29
Demography and Settlement Pattern	32
Village Economy	33
Early Gurung Economy	33
Recent Trends	35
Contemporary Ghaisu Economy	38
CHAPTER 3: INTERACTION GROUPS AND MARRIAGE	45
The Local Lineage	45
Fictive Kinship	46
Youth Associations	49
Marriage in Ghaisu	54

THE PRINCIPAL UNION	57
The arranged marriage	57
In an elopement	61
SUBSIDIARY UNION	62
A subsidiary union of substitution	62
The cohabitation variety	63

CHAPTER 4: SOCIAL AND RELIGIOUS CELEBRATIONS — 66

Introduction	66
The Celebration of Dasai	66
Ghanto: Gurung Dance-Drama	71
The Non-Hindu Ritual Specialists of Ghaisu	76
Sora Jat Shamans	77
Astrologers	80
Buddhist Lamas	80
Contractural Relations between Ritualists and Clients	83
THE CELEBRATION OF DEATH	84
Initial Mortuary Rites	86
The Period of Transition	95
The Commemorative Rites of Pai (Arghun)	97
The Prestations of Amel	101

CHAPTER 5: JAT INTERFACE - CONFLICT AND CHANGE — 104

Introduction and Overview	104
Recent Political Developments	107
Crisis Development	111
CHANGES IN FESTIVAL INTERACTIONS	112
Dasai	112
Ghanto	113
BREACH OF ENDOGAMY	114
REORGANIZATION OF RODI	118
THE BREAKDOWN OF FICTIVE KINSHIP	123
CATEGORIES OF LABOR AND SERVICES	124
CHANGING LAYMAN-RITUALIST RELATIONSHIPS	127
CHANGES IN FUNERARY CEREMONIES	129
Conflict Control and Reintegration	131
COMPARTMENTALIZATION	132
AMELIORATION: AN EPILOGUE	133

GLOSSARY	136
BIBLIOGRAPHY	147

List of Illustrations

Photographs

1.	Gurung porters on a mountain track	7
2.	Gurung man dancing the *serga kwe*	8
3.	A view from Gurung country - the Himalayas	15
4.	Ploughing with bullocks and wooden plough	15
5, 6.	Gurung house building	19
7.	A highland Gurung village under snow	25
8.	A valley village amidst corn fields	25
9, 10.	Gurung men slaughtering a water buffalo	37
11.	Non-Gurung horn-blowers	55
12.	The groom, seated with men of his patrilineage.	55
13.	A noted dancer from a neighbouring village	59
14.	Wedding feast	60
15.	The rite of *tho seba*.	67
16.	The shrine of the goddess Durga	70
17.	Girl dancers of Ghanto in their costume	72
18.	The ritual gesture of obeisance called *syo laba*	74
19.	The clowns of Ghanto entertain the crowd	75
20.	The author with a clown	75
21, 22.	Gurung *khepre* shamans	78
23.	Gurung lamas reciting	81
24.	A white flag is raised over the deceased's house	88
25.	Shamans performing their ritual	88
26.	The shaman guru performing the ritual of *o nob*	89
27.	The funeral procession	89
28.	Shamans purchacing a place in the cemetry for the deceased	90
29.	Sons-in-law prepare the funeral pyre	90
30.	Head shaving at the funeral	91
31.	Visiting lamas	92
32.	Young village lamas	93
33.	Young boy mimics his elders	94

Maps

Map 1	Nepal and Central Gurung Country	3
Map 2	Ghaisu Village and Besi Hamlet	26

Tables

Table 1	Gurung Speakers in Ten Districts	1
2	The Char Jat Clans	5
3	Demography of Ghaisu Village (1972), Gurung	39
4	The Six Wealthiest Householders, Ghaisu (1972)	40
5	Soldiers Among the 26 Wealthiest Households, Ghaisu (1972)	41
6	Grain Production by Clan and Jat, Ghaisu (1972)	41
7	Rodi Membership in Ghaisu Before and After 1970	119

Figures

Figure 1	Lamichane Clan Genealogy, Ghaisu Village	30
2	Fictive Kinship Bonds in Ghaisu	47
3	Char Jat Marriage Rules, Western Gurung	54
4	Char Jat Marriage Rules, Central Gurung	56
5	Affinal Relationships in Preferred Matrilateral Cross-Cousin Marriage	87
6	Affinal Relationships in a Non-Matrilateral Marriage	87
7	The Plan of the *pla* Effigy (adapted from Pignede 1966: 348)	98
8	Flow of Prestations from *mo* to Wife's Patrilineage in Hypergamous Union	117

Legends

Legend 1	Gurung Genealogy as Published by Pignede (1962)	10
1a	Gurung Genealogy from Lamjung Village Version	10
2	Defeat of the Ghale Raja	16
2a	Defeat of the Ghale Raja, Alternate Version (Conclusion)	16
3	Early History of Ghaisu	29
4	Origins of the Image of Durga in Ghaisu	69
5	Origins of the Char Jat Ritual Contract in Ghaisu	83

Preface

This book has two purposes. One is to give an ethnographic description of the Gurungs of the Nepal Himalaya, with particular attention to social and political organization and the interaction of kin and non-kin based groups of villagers. The other purpose is to discuss conflict and change among contemporary Gurungs of one village, bearing in mind the traditional norms and styles of personal and group interaction and statuses which are in many ways unique to the Gurungs.

The Gurungs of Nepal have been generally considered an ethnic group known for its internal social cohesion and unity, despite marked social cleavages, as well as for an ability to work well together in a variety of chores despite disparate economic and political conditions between persons. It was with some interest, then, that in the initial stages of my ethnographic field studies of the Gurungs in 1971 I detected serious interpersonal and group conflict on the inside of village social life. The conflict strained the façade of serenity by which the Gurungs appear to the outsider. Although I focused my attentions primarily on Gurung life and culture in Ghaisu, a mountain village in the Lamjung Himal of central Nepal, I was able to discern through encounters with Gurungs in other villages, in Gurung legend and geneologies, and in reading the only other extensive studies of Gurung society then available (Pignede 1962, 1966; Macfarlane 1972) a built-in conflict throughout the tribe. The conflict is one inherent in a dual social organization consisting of two Gurung sub-tribes called the Sora Jat and the Char Jat, each comprised of many clans and lineages. It is rooted in historical precedent and exacerbated by contemporary economic and political contingencies. I determined early in my fieldwork to uncover those elements of Gurung social life which explained unity despite duality, and ultimately to examine conflict between the sub-tribes in Ghaisu in light of both tradition and modernity.

Ghaisu is an isolated and relatively traditional mountain village in the foothills of the Lamjung Himal, an eastern extension of the more famous Annapurna Himalayan massif of central Nepal. The village is located within the sphere of socio-economic and political influence of Ghanpokhara, the largest Gurung village of the region (Map 1, p. 3). Other Gurungs consider Ghaisu to be a bit 'old-fashioned' perhaps. In recent years, changes outside of Ghaisu within the larger Nepali national system have infringed upon traditional village life in a few far-reaching ways. These influences reflect the nation's quest for modernity, as well as an historical trend of Hinduization throughout the hills (see Caplan 1970).

Recent changes at the national level have affected contemporary life and have contributed to conflict and change in Ghaisu village life as I observed it.

The research for this book was conducted under the auspices of the U.S. Public Health Service's National Institutes of Health [Grant No. 5 TO1 GMO 1382 07 (BHS)] through the Department of Anthropology, University of Oregon. This book represents an edited and revised version of my 1974 dissertation. I am endebted to the National Institutes of Health, to my mentors and colleagues at the University of Oregon, and to my present employers, Abt Associates, Inc., of Cambridge, Massachusetts, for their combined help, time, and consideration during the preparation of this study.

Field studies were conducted for fourteen months in 1971 and 1972. Much of the book discusses ethno-historical traditions dating back several centuries, but those parts dealing with contemporary conflict and change may be generally ascribed to the period 1970-1972, when intra-village conflict was intense. The bulk of the data were derived from observation while my wife, Kareen, and I were resident in the village. I was also fortunate to have employed two Gurung research assistants, Mr. Komal Ghaley of Tilje village, for three months, and Mr. Nareshwar (Naresh) Jang Gurung of Ghanpokhara, for ten months. Together we are sincerely appreciative of the villagers for their forebearance, warm hospitality, and remarkable tolerance during our stay in Ghaisu.

A word about my research assistants and their important roles in the research and life of Ghaisu village. Both Komal and Naresh maintained remarkable rapport with our hosts, despite a number of personal circumstances and aspirations which appeared, at the outset, to be liabilities, not assets. By virtue of a combination of birth, marriage, and education, however, these men were able to walk the thin line between outsiders - suspect and aloof - and insiders - uncomfortably close to the conflict; they fitted between the two extremes, in a special category of 'marginal men,' more in than out, while they lived and collected data with me in the village.

Komal and Naresh are men of high and very visible status in Gurung society. Both are college graduates, with the attendant life styles that clearly differentiate them as urbanized, modernized Nepalis. Both studied economics and political science at the university, and both are fluent in Gurung, Nepali, and English. Their tri-lingualism was of considerable help to me when it came to translating recorded interviews and social events, and in determining the precise meaning of Gurung idiom. As Naresh is a Lamichane clansman, and Komal a Ghale, they share in the high status of the Char Jat sub-tribe. Neither have Char Jat relatives in Ghaisu, but are considered to be jat 'brothers' by fellow Char Jat clansmen everywhere. Furthermore, Naresh and Komal are cousins (Komal's mother is Naresh's father's sister) as well as brothers-in-law (Komal married Naresh's sister), and hence they share both kinship and affinity to the famous Gurung Subbas of Ghanpokhara who earlier this century held predominant economic and political power in the region (Messerschmidt and Gurung 1974).

Their common bond of brotherhood to the Char Jat of Ghaisu is complemented by an analogous bond to the Sora Jat clansmen of the village through the institution of *mit* (or *ngyel*, discussed in Chapter 3), a form of blood brotherhood across sub-tribal lines. Given the extensive generalization of *mit* relations and a large measure of obligatory reciprocity between *mit-* 'brothers' however far removed, they were brought into close contact with the Sora Jat faction (specifically the Yoj clan) in the Ghaisu intra-village conflict. Their *mit* relationship is through an affine (in-law) of the Subba lineage to a Sora Jat man who has relatives in Ghaisu.

These two loose fraternal relationships with both jats in the village afforded both Komal and Naresh ample opportunity to act as sympathetic listeners, and at times, as respected advisers, to both sides of the controversy. Finally, both assistants resided in the homes of key men in our study, men who figured importantly at the center of the conflict. This gave them special access to the insiders' perspective. Naresh's host, a Nasi clansman, was particularly important in this regard, in that he eventually became a leader in ameliorating the conflict under circumstances described in the Epilogue.

A Note on Foreign Terms and Quotations.

Some Gurung and Nepali terms are italicized in the text, in a form which is close to their proper pronunciation. Others are treated as if they were English. All foreign terms are transcribed in the Glossary (pp. 136-146) according to accepted linguistic style.

Although Gurung is an unwritten language, these terms were recorded in the field in the same devanagri script that is used for Nepali. Transliteration from the devanagri to romanized spellings was done according to a system adapted from the Summer Institute of Linguistics systems for Gurung (Glover 1971) and for Nepali (Hari 1971; see also Turner 1965). Tibetan terms are rendered after Jäschke (1881).

Definitions of terms are given as informants interpreted them to me and my assistants. In addition for Nepali, dictionaries by both Turner (1965) and Sharma (1962) were consulted, and for Tibetan terms, the dictionary by Jäschke (1881).

Place names, with the exception of a few pseudonyms where indicated, are spelled essentially as they are found on the Survey of India maps of Nepal.

Several passages in the book are quoted in French from Bernard Pignede's *Les Gurungs* (1966), followed by the English translation. The only full length translation of *Les Gurungs* into English is a rough, unpublished manuscript prepared by Alan and Gillian Macfarlane. Translations in the book have been adapted from the Macfarlane version with certain changes to better represent the original meaning. Permission to use the Macfarlanes' work is kindly acknowledged, although responsibility for the correctness of the translations is my own.

Acknowledgements.

Permission to quote passages in the text of the book from each of the following sources has been granted by the copyright holders as indicated:

- from Francis (Hamilton) Buchanan, *An Account of the Kingdom of Nepal* (1819; 1971, New Delhi; Manjusri), copyright (C) 1971 by H. K. Kulöy, Kathmandu.

- from Bernard Pignede, "Clan Organization and Hierarchy among the Gurungs," *Contributions to Indian Sociology,* volume 6 (1962), pages 102-119, copyright (C) 1962 by Mouton & Co., The Hague.

- from Bernard Pignede, *Les Gurungs* (1966, The Hague: Mouton), copyright (C) 1966 by Mouton & Co., The Hague.

I am also grateful to Dr. Alan D. J. Macfarlane for permission to quote passages from *Population and Economy in Central Nepal* (Ph. D. Dissertation, University of London, 1972), and to the India Office Library and Records, London, for access to and the quotation of excerpts from Brian H. Hodgson's unpublished handwritten miscellaneous notes on the Gurungs of Nepal, volume 5 (n.d.), pages 9-12, 44-45, 75-78.

Special debts of gratitude are due to my two field assistants, to the villagers of Ghaisu, to Dor Bahadur Bista and Dr. Harka Bahadur Gurung both of Kathmandu, to the officers and staff of the Institute of Nepal and Asian Studies, Tribhuvan University/Kirtipur, and to others in the service of His Majesty's Government of Nepal who helped my wife and me in many ways. Finally, I wish to give special thanks and appreciation to my wife, Kareen 'Maya', for her fortitude good spirit, and strong support throughout the period of research and writing.

CHAPTER ONE
The Gurungs of Nepal

Introduction

The Gurungs are a people of Mongoloid physical stock who migrated to the southern slopes of the Himalaya in central Nepal many centuries ago. Like similar Tibeto-Burman speaking tribes, such as their neighbours the Magars, Tamangs, and Thakali, the Gurungs live at the interstices between two great cultural and social traditions, Indian Hinduism and Tibetan Buddhism, and between two distinct ecological zones, the low sub-tropical valleys and the alpine mountain highlands. At the present time, their life and culture is poised between long and steady tradition and the changes which accompany modernity.

The Gurungs traditionally dwell in the foothills of the Annapurna and Lamjung Himalaya and Himal Chuli, in districts within and adjacent to Gandaki Zone (Table 1).

TABLE 1
Gurung Speakers in Ten District

(1971 Nepal Census)

Zone	District	Gurung Speakers	Total Population	Gurung Percentage
Gandaki	Lamjung	36,742	140,226	26.0%
	Syangja	25,620	258,606	9.5%
	Kaski	25,466	151,749	16.8%
	Gorkha	20,781	178,265	11.7%
	Tanahu	13,031	158,139	8.2%
	Parbat	9,799	118,689	8.0%
	Manang	3,699	7,436	50.0%
Dhaulagiri	Mustang	3,279	26,944	12.0%
Bagmati	Dhading	8,028	236,276	3.0%
Narayani	Chitwan	6,355	183,644	3.5%

The number of Gurung speakers in Nepal has been set at 171,609 according to the official 1971 Nepal Census. This is approximately 1.5% of the entire Nepalese population of nearly 12 million, and is an increase of nearly 14,000 Gurung speakers since the 1961 Consus was taken. Bear in mind that the figures indicate only those Gurungs who registered with the Census as "speakers of Gurung as mother tongue," hence they give no indication of ethnic Gurungs who registered as Nepali speakers. [1]

Gurung speakers are found in every district of the country, but the majority dwell in Lamjung, Kaski, Gorkha, Tanahu, Parbat, and Syangja. Chitwan's 6,355 Gurung speakers represent recent migration to the newly opened settlement areas of the Rapti Valley. Migration to other districts, particularly in East Nepal, dates in part as far back as the Gorkha Conquest and related events of the 18th and early 19th centuries A.D. Districts in the east and south reporting 1,000 or more Gurung speakers are Kathmandu (1,102), Rupendehi (1,321), Sankhuwasabha (1,618), Illam (1,709), and Taplejung (1,884).

Early Gurung religion was animistic and shamanic, akin to the pre-Buddhist Bon religion of Tibet. The economy was herding, hunting, and swidden (slash and burn) agriculture adapted to the rugged highlands and high forests. Gurungs also have an early tradition of trans-Himalayan trading (Hodgson n.d.). In recent centuries, they have been in contact with Hindu migrants from the south led by the aggressive and militant Rajputs of the Kshatriya caste of India (Chhetri in Nepal). The Nepalese Hindu castes of Brahman and Chhetri eventually came to dominate the hill people culturally, politically, and economically. Nepali, a Sanskritic language, became the lingua franca and it is used today by the Gurungs and other hills people wherever they interact with Hindu caste populations, primarily at markets and in the context of government administration. Sedentary agriculture based on irrigated and upland rice as well as on maize, wheat, eleusine, millet, and barley has become the economic mainstay of the hill people. In the northerly parts of their region, some Gurungs still pursue seasonal highland grazing with herds of sheep, goats, cattle, and water buffalo. The Gurungs of eastern Manang District herd yak instead of water buffalo. Gurungs still engage in long distance trade. Until recently they bartered with Tibetan salt traders to their north. Now they mostly trade in the monetary economy with Nepalese and Indian merchants at their south.[2]

The Gurung tribe can be broadly categorized into southern or lower hillsmen and northern highlanders. The highland, or *lekhali* Gurungs retain a life style more closely tied to older traditions, particularly to the degree that they still pursue high altitude pastoralism. In contrast, the Gurungs of the lower hills reveal significant accommodation to Hindu cultural systems.

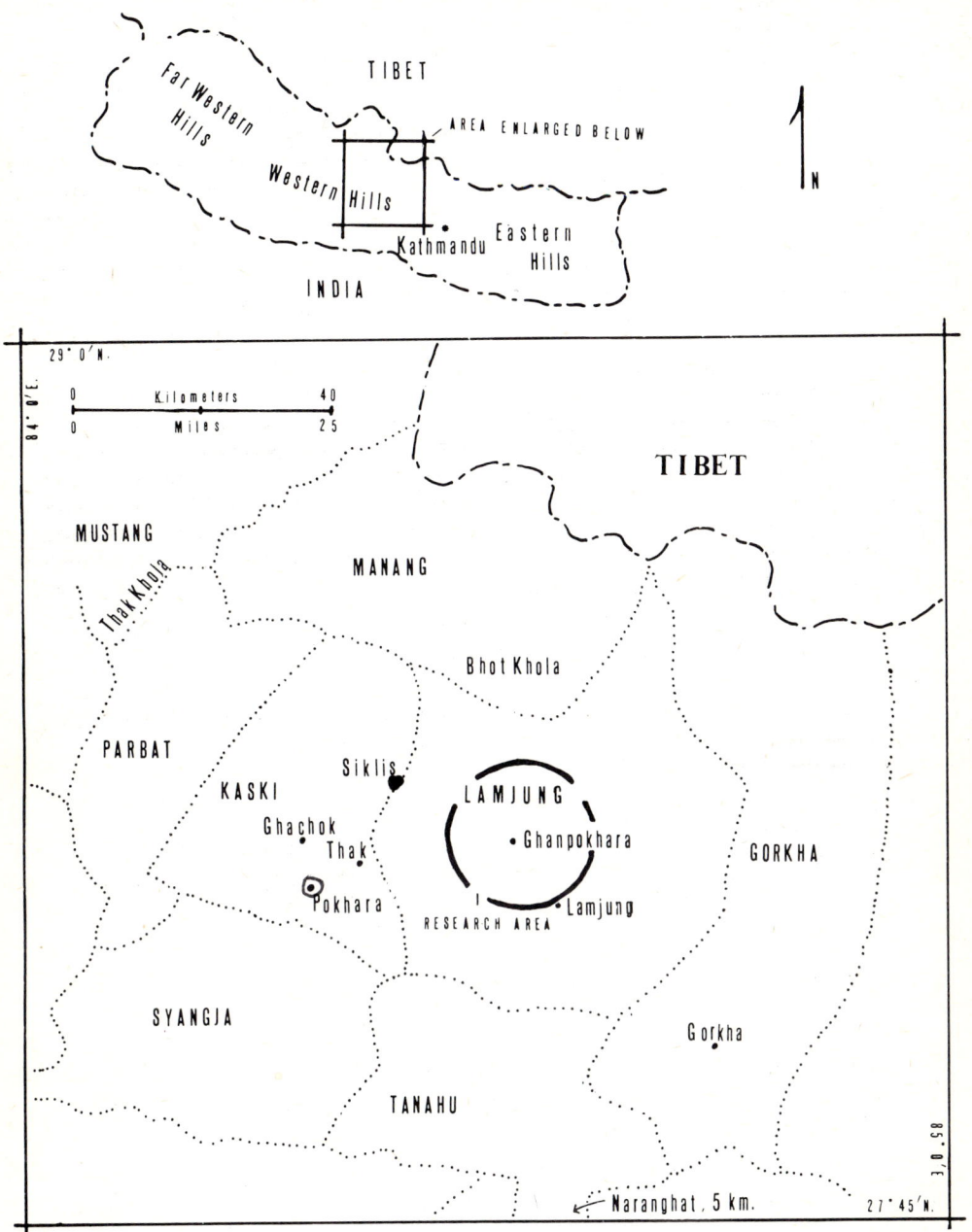

Map 1. Nepal and Central Gurung Country

The Gurung tribe can also be logically and conveniently categorized into the 'western Gurungs' who dwell in Kaski, and in the adjacent districts of Syangja and Parbat; the 'central Gurungs' who dwell in Lamjung and adjacent Tanahu and eastern Manang Districts; and the 'eastern Gurungs' of Gorkha and adjacent Dhading Districts.[3] This Gurung trichotomy conforms with long-standing geo-political considerations, with minor cultural differences, and with primary linguistic differences.

Warren Glover and John Landon (1975, personal communications) identify three distinct linguist types among the Gurungs:

(1) The Western Gurung dialect. Its communicative center is in Kaski District, and it is heard spoken as far east as the western edge of Lamjung District.

(2) The Eastern Gurung dialect. Its communicative center is in Lamjung District, in what I have categorized above as 'central Gurung' territory. The eastern dialect is heard, as well, in western Gorkha District.

(3) The Ghale language. It is heard east of the Darondi River in Gorkha District. This is not considered a dialect of Gurung, but is a language as "radically more different from the true Gurung than either Tamang, Thakali, or Manang . . all of which are certainly regarded as separate languages" (Glover and Landon, *ibid.*). Note, however, that the Ghale clansmen who live among central and western Gurungs speak Gurung dialects, not Ghale. The Gurungs of Ghaisu and vicinity, discussed in this book, are central Gurungs and speak the Eastern Gurung dialect.[4]

Gurung Social Organization[5]

The distinctive structural feature of Gurung society is its dual organization into two hierarchical strata or sub-tribes called the Char Jat or 'four clans' and the Sora Jat or 'sixteen clans.' Each jat is endogamous; that is, members are obliged to marry within their own jat. Both incorporate a number of named patrilineal clans which are exogamous, whereby one is required to marry outside the clan. The clans are, in turn, segmented into local lineages. Jat endogamy and clan exogamy are the most important features of the social order, and every Gurung inherits the clan and jat of his/her father.

'Char Jat' and 'Sora Jat' are Nepali terms, widely used in the society. The numbers 'four' and 'sixteen' are not entirely accurate, but are important in terms of status distinctions. The Char Jat are of allegedly superior status to the Sora Jat.[6,7]

4

The Char Jat Clans. Within the Char Jat there are four clans, which have a hierarchical order of their own. They are commonly called, in order from high to low ranking, the Ghale, Ghodane, Lama, and Lamichane clans. (Other terms are given in Table 2). Gurung and Nepali terms are used interchangeably. All but the Ghodane clan are found in Ghaisu village.

TABLE 2
The Char Jat Clans

Nepali	Western Gurung	Central Gurung
Ghale	Ghale	Kle
Ghodane	Kon	Kon
Lama	Lama	Lam
Lamichane	Plon, Lem, Pai	Lem, Khhro

Tribal legend, conferring this traditional order to the clan, reflects a four-fold hierarchy common to a number of Himalayan tribes (Allen 1973). The following discussion points out certain differences in occupational roles and in social status distinctions observed among the Gurungs of northern Lamjung District, at Ghaisu and vicinity.

The Ghale, or *kle,* are by tradition a clan of ancient kings of paramount chiefs. *Kle* is derived from *khle,* an old Gurung term meaning 'master, lord, chief, king,' and heard most often in a religious context to refer to the lord of the birds, keeper of the cemetary, or a shaman's patron deity. Most Ghale clansmen live in central and eastern Gurung country, in the districts of Lamjung and Gorkha.

A 'Ghale Raja,' an ancestral Gurung king described in legends, is said to have reigned over the original Gurung kingdom centered in what is now northern Lamjung District.[8] He was overthrown by the Nepali Raja of the Principality of Lamjung, probably around the 15th Century A.D. The site of an early residence of the Ghale Raja is said to be Khhol, an abandoned village site high in the forest of northern Lamjung (Messerschmidt n.d.). Some informants refer to Khhol as the first Gurung village south of the Himalaya.

The Ghodane, or *kon,* are the least well known of the Char Jat clans. Pignede offers a very tentative hypothesis linking both terms to the Tibetan *mgon* meaning 'lord,' as well as to '*go-gnas,* 'official position,' and '*go-pa,* 'village head.' He adds that "according to Gurung tradition, the *kon* were administrators of the *ghale* kings. Today, many village chiefs belong to the *kon* clan" (1962: 108-109). Pignede speaks from observations among western Gurungs where the Ghodane are

5

numerous and the Lamichane few. Among the central Gurungs of my study, however, Ghodane clansmen were not encountered. In their place, the Lamichane predominate and are traditionally accorded the high position as chief ministers to the former Ghale kings, despite their last place in the Char Jat hierarchy. Hence, this data conflicts with certain legendary authority with Pignede's account (1962, 1966), and subsequently with Allen's recent analysis of a four-fold hierarchical homology among Himalayan tribes (1973). The conflict may represent relatively recent changes in the status of the Lamichane clan.

The Lama, or *lam* clan, undoubtedly takes its name from the Tibetan *bla-ma,* 'the higher, upper, superior one,' or generally, 'priest.' Lama clan legend tells that the other Char Jat Gurungs migrated from the north and were followed somewhat later by Buddhist lamas who settled among them in northern Lamjung. In time the clan of Lama became recognized as a Gurung clan of hereditary ritualists employed primarily by the Char Jat. In the past, and to a limited extent today, Lama clansmen have taken religious training under the tutelage of Tibetan Buddhist lamas in centers of religious learning in Tibet and in the Nepal-Tibet border regions (for example, at Nar in Manang District). Today, relatively few Lama clansmen pursue the strict classical Tibetan monastic education of their forefathers, although they still claim their ritual status and rights. Buddhism among the Gurungs in general is waning in the face of inroads by Hinduism; it is still strong, however, among the more northerly villages which are isolated from the mainstream of Nepali life and where traditionalism is valued more highly. Ghaisu is one of those villages.

The Lamichane clan is called by a number of terms in Gurung, including *khhro* and *lem* in northern Lamjung, and *lem, plon,*[9] and *pai* in Kaski and Parbat Districts (Pignede 1962, 1966). *Khhro* was probably substituted for the older term *lem* under the circumstances of Lamichane clan ascendency to predominance in village chieftenships in recent generations. Apparently in the west, the term *khhro* (or *kroh)* is reserved for the 'chief of the village' who is frequently a member of the Ghodane clan. To make matters even more confusing, in local central Gurung tradition the Lamichane are also said to have occupied the ministerial role ascribed to the Ghodane by Pignede's account.

A widely known and perhaps the oldest of traditions, places the Lamichane in a fourth rank position subordinate to the Lama clan. Today, among central Gurungs, specifically at Ghanpokhara, Ghaisu, and in neighboring villages, many village chiefs (*khhro, mukhya*) are Lamichane clansmen. Simultaneously, they are also the local land revenue functionaries (*jimuwal*). They obtained and have maintained these roles by hereditary succession with the apparent support of the House of Gorkha, the ruling dynasty of Nepal which traces its origins to the ancient

1. Gurung porters on a mountain track

2. Gurung man dancing the *serga kwe* during the funerary memorial ceremonies, drumming the *dhandu* bass drum

Nepali Raja of Lamjung.

The Sora Jat. While there are indeed only four clans within the Char Jat, as the name implies, there are far more than the indicated sixteen Sora Jat clans. Pignede (1962) records 36 clans and more are found listed in the writings of Vansittart (1916), Hodgson (1884) and other early writers. The Sora Jat of Ghaisu village are represented by eight Sora Jat clans: Kromche, Nasi, Ngor, Pajyu, Phle, Thorche, Tu, and Yoj. There is no discernible hierarchical ordering within the Sora Jat clans, although in any one locality the more populous and/or most wealthy take precedence in most instances. Little can be said about ancient occupational roles ascribed to the Sora Jat clans, although there are vague references to one clan or the other having engaged in what are now considered ritually defiling forms of manual labor. Nepali caste groups now perform the low caste and untouchable occupations needed for the smooth running of the village economy; some reside in Gurung villages or are contracted for their services from villages at a distance. The Sora Jat as a whole, however, is said to have been obliged to perform in roles subservient to the higher status Char Jat, and this becomes the focal point of a long discussion later in the book.

Tribal Hierarchy: The Basis of Social Conflict

A fundamental social conflict which exists throughout Gurung society is based on the question of relative superiority or inferiority of Char Jat and Sora Jat status. Because of the dominant role this conflict holds among Gurungs generally, and the special role played by the Char Jat Lamichane clan in particular, it is necessary to investigate legendary authority for hierarchy at two levels: (1) the dual hierarchy of the two Gurung jats, and (2) the four-fold hierarchy that exists within the Char Jat. The rise of the Lamichane clan to most favored status in northern Lamjung District is best understood in these contexts.

Dual Hierarchy of the Jats. A pseudo-history of the Gurungs is found in a document called the Gurung Genealogy (*gurung-ko vamsavali*) which is well known among Gurungs. Several versions of the document exist, one of which has been published in Nepali, with parts of it published subsequently in English and French by Pignede (1962, 1966). Nearly identical hand-written texts exist in the villages. One such text, which appears to be a rewriting in modern Nepali of an older document dated 1694 V.S. (1637 A.D.), was found in a Lamjung District village. That older document is probably prior to the published version. Because the basic legend is important to the study, the published version and the village version are quoted verbatim and side by side below for comparison. The first two paragraphs are virtually identical in both versions. Beginning with paragraph three, however, significant differences occur. Some parts of Pignede's published version are apparently and inexplicably missing, or are only paraphrased. This is most noticeable in the concluding paragraphs of the legend where Pignede's own dotted lines indicate his omissions.

LEGEND 1	LEGEND 1a
Gurung Genealogy as Published by Pignede (1962)	*Gurung Genealogy from Lamjung Village Version*

The king of Kaski asked his Brahman priest to explain to him the origin of the Gurungs and of the Carjat (sic) and Solahjat (sic) divisions. This is what the Brahman told him:

"

There was a king of gotra Bharadvaja who belonged to *Sūryajā* dynasty. He had two sons. The elder, Locan, was not loved by his parents while Nocan, the younger, was their favourite. They disobeyed the rule of succession, crowned the younger son and neglected the elder son. Locan was much grieved and began to doubt the worth of worldly possessions. One day he left the palace and went towards the Himalaya where he wished to lead an ascetic life. He was accompanied by his wife Kali and his priest, the son of Mukunda Acharye, of gotra Garga. The latter had with him his wife Kasi. The group included also a slave, Kesai Singh of Khowase, and his wife Phali. On their way they met two prostitutes and spent the night under the same shelter with them. While the prince and the priest were asleep, the two prostitutes broke their *janae* (brahmanical cord), poured wine on their lips and fled. When the prince and the priest awoke, they realized their disgrace. Henceforth they could no longer belong to their castes. They settled in the Himalaya and hollowed out a cave to live in . . . One day they said to the slave: "You have always been faithful. From this day you will no longer be a slave. Your name will be Ker Singh Thapa and we shall eat the food that you prepare. The Himalayan mountains are pure. Here we may eat the food of

"

"

"

"

"

"

10

a man of inferior caste . . ." The princess had three sons: Ghale Mahan Gurung, Ghotane Mahan Gurung, Lama Mahan Gurung, and a daughter, Lakshmi. The priest's wife had two sons, Lamechane Mahan Gurung, the elder, and Plone Lamechane Gurung, the younger, and three daughters, Kumari, Nari, and Mali. Later the prince's children married the priest's children. The prince's sons were the first *ghale, ghotane* and *lama* and the priest's sons were the first *lamechane*. Thus appeared four Carjat clans. They were named Mahan for their ability to meditate. Ker Singh's wife had ten daughters and sixteen sons who were named: Pajgyu Thapa, Nor Thapa, Kepcae Thapa, Timce Thapa, Procae Thapa, Yoca Thapa, Khulal Thapa, Kromcae Thapa, Gabri Thapa, Dorsae Thapa, Bhaecae Thapa, Kokae Thapa, Kucae Thapa, Namcae Thapa, Leṅae Thapa, Rupcae Thapa. They founded the sixteen Solahjat clans. The brothers and sisters intermarried.

A man of the *namcae* clan (Solahjat) took advantage of a *ghotane* girl.

The Solahjat begged forgiveness so that the Carjat would not kill the man:

"We shall be your servants, sweeping your way and sprinkling dew on it, walking behind carrying your load and shoes, eating your left-overs . . ."

,,

,,

,,

,,

A son named Namche Thawa (sic, Thapa? Sora Jat) took advantage of the Char Jat daughter of the Ghodane. Her name was Marphi. All of the Char Jat Mahagurus gathered together saying: "We are of the royal family of Rajputra and you are the sons of the servant (*dasi putra*). Because you have taken advantage of her, we must kill you." And they took up the sword in their hands to kill him. But all of the Sora Jat gathered together and said: "We are the sons of servants. We have made a mistake, have mercy on us. We sixteen brothers (*sora bhai*) will go ahead of you four brothers (*char bhai*) and sweep away your left-overs, and walking behind you we will carry your load, and whatever you order us to do that we will do for you. At your marriage we will carry the palaquin. At your wedding our girls will carry your *kalas*[10] and whoever carries the *kalas* will be decorated with fine clothes and ornaments, and will take the fees paid for these services. We promise to do all this if you will not kill our brother Namche." Then the Char Jat did not kill him.

The parents, Lochan and Ker Singh and the priest Bali Acharya got together and had a discussion. "The Char Jat are the sons of the princes and the Sora Jat are the sons of the servant. Therefore intermarriage shall be prohibited. If a Char Jat man has (sexual) relations with a Sora Jat woman he will be absolved of fault, but if a Sora Jat man has relations with a Char Jat woman, then a fine of Rs.16 will be charged." And, having promised to abide by all these things, from that day forward they had to pay the fine.

... Intermarriage was prohibited. However a Carjat man might without fault get a Solahjat woman but the reverse would be punished ...

Lochan and Bali Acharya threw a trident (*trishul*) at the Himalaya and from that place (where it fell) they took their food and ate (i.e. settled). Afterwards all of their sons came from Kailash (the high Himalaya, or Tibet) to the forest of Lamjung and established there a Ghale Raja from the Ghale Mahaguru.

the population increasing they moved to the Lamjung area and made the elder Ghale their king.

Many years later that Ghale Raja fought with the Sahi Raja of Nuwakot and the Ghale Raja lost. Since then, the name Mahaguru was lost, and the name Gurung was given in its place. At that time, too, the Sora Jat were set free to live as they wished, but they chose to live with the Char Jat. This was because the Sahi Raja had killed their brothers, therefore, they said: "We will live with these Char Jat wherever they go, and follow them, and serve them, and respect them." This was their promise.

The king Sahi of Nowakot defeated the Ghale king but the Solahjat insisted on remaining with the Carjat. They settled in Lamjung, Kaski, Ghandrung ...

After that, the Sahi Raja returned to his own palace. In this way they became Gurung. This is what Bhoj Raj *purohit* (personal priest) Brahman told to the Kaski Raja Jagdish Khana. This was written in the year 1694 V.S. on the ninth day of the month of Phagun, on a Monday (i.e. February 1637 A.D.).

There are several important but conflicting elements to the legend. For one, the Char Jat progenitors are alternately traced to India in the South, which implies high status, while their sons come from Kailash, in the North, which does not. It is sometimes assumed that reference to the Rajputra implies descent from the Rajput clans of Rajputana in India. Some contemporary Char Jat Gurungs firmly believe this, and my Char Jat assistant initially interpreted the handwritten text to me as such. However, in the hand-written village text, the Char Jat "of the royal family of Rajputra" are placed opposite in status to the Sora Jat of the family of "the sons of the servant", an opposition which may be more reasonably interpreted as being merely between high status 'royal sons' (*raj putra*) and low status 'servants' sons' (*dasi putra*) with no clear reference to ultimate geographical or more specific genealogical origins.

Another conflicting element is that the Sora Jat, which at first is classed as subservient, is then seemingly absolved of that low status. In any case, the perspective is from the dominant Hindu caste system introduced into Nepal by migrants from the south.

The legend is an attempt to resolve two conflicts in cultural accommodation caused by the anomaly of an otherwise egalitarian tribal entity in contact with the dominant and hierarchical Nepali Hindu caste system. It has two messages. One is about intra-Gurung hierarchy. The legend is a status-legitimizing document, a symbol of high rank by which the Char Jat can support their claims of superiority vis-a-vis the Sora Jat. Its second message is that the Gurungs in general were originally in an hierarchy commensurate with certain other high Hindu castes.

Allen (1973) refers to this legend as "an example of the common type of myth in which a Himalayan group tries to raise its status by claiming an origin among the purer Hindus to the south." But there is some question as to whether the Gurungs themselves originally perpetrated the myth, or whether it was put upon them by others. The legend has great importance to non-Gurungs; that is, to the caste society. Pignede quotes a Sora Jat reaction to the legend from Siklis village in Kaski District. "The discrimination was created by the Brahmans and the Southerners to divide the Gurungs and give them inferior standing in Nepalese society" (1962: 119). This observation is reasonable, for the genealogy is clearly a contrived explanation of Gurung origins and social status.[11]

Besides this legendary authority, a precedent of official declaration of Char Jat superiority is also said to exist in an historical example of administrative fiat. The following account is generally well known by the Gurungs (Pignede 1962: 116):

During the second half of the 19th century ... the Chief Minister [Jang Bahadur Rana] of Nepal was called upon to judge whether the Solahjat were of inferior status to the Carjat. In a long document, supporting his argument with data taken from several Nepalese legends, Jang Bahadur answered in the affirmative and specified that the difference of status between Carjat and Solahjat was perfectly founded.

In northern Lamjung District, Jang Bahadur's decision is remembered only in this saying (in Nepali): *aphno aphno jatma aphai thula chha, tara sanatan dharma mannera khau* ('in one's own jat one is superior, but one must eat honoring ancient duty'). The last part of the saying is considered by Char Jat informants to be sufficient justification for their claim to superiority, by ancient duty or tradition. On the other hand, Sora Jat clansmen refer to the first phrase to argue that superiority is relevant only within, not between, jats. Whether accurately reconstructed or not (but true and authoritative as far as the villagers are concerned) the saying neither proves nor solves anything, but like the legend, is open to manipulation.[12]

Four-fold Hierarchy and Lamichane Ascendancy. Legends 1 and 1a suggest that the Lamichane progenitors had a low status within the Char Jat and may have had certain priestly origins. Local tradition in northern Lamjung, however, implies that the Lamichane have long held high status within the Char Jat by filling a ministerial role immediately subordinate to the former Ghale king(s). Today, many Lamichane clansmen are village chiefs and land revenue collectors, offices of high status and prestige which have been hereditarily maintained by patrilineal succession for many generations. Several prominent Lamichane lineages, particularly in the village of Ghanpokhara, have more recently risen to the very pinnacle of contemporary Gurung social hierarchy to positions of superior economic and political power and leadership.[13]

If the assumption of initial low status is correct - - and a certain homology between several neighboring Himalayan tribes with similar four-fold structural features seems to support it (Allen 1973) - - how is the successful ascendancy of the Lamichane clan explained?

The question turns specifically on how Lamichane clansmen succeeded in winning the favor of the Nepali government; that is, of the House of Gorkha, during the early formative period of that dynasty. Part of the answer may be found in a sketchy legend told in various forms by Ghale, Lamichane, and Lama informants of northern Lamjung and southeast Manang Districts. Legend 2, below, elaborates the fall of the last Ghale Raja at the hands of the Nepali Raja of Lamjung (who was in the patri-line of the Raja of Nuwakot referred to in Legends 1

3. A view from Gurung country - the Himalayas

4. Ploughing with bullocks and wooden plough, with woman sowing seed behind

and 1a), progenitor of the House of Gorkha. This event probably occurred during or shortly after the 15th century A.D. when the Lamjung Raja was consolidating his power in Lamjung and Gorkha Districts. He was, at that time, one of the most powerful of the 'twenty-four kings' (*chaubisi raja*) of West Nepal (Hasrat 1970: 111; Stiller 1973).

LEGEND 2

Defeat of the Ghale Raja

There was a Ghale Raja of Pauchok whose chief minister was a Lamichane. The Lamichane requested the Raja's daughter in marriage for his son. The Raja agreed on the condition that the Lamichane choose his daughter from among all the girls fetching water at the water spout. The Raja then sent a servant girl dressed in fine clothes in the place of his daughter and tricked the Lamichane. This was the cause of the quarrel between the Lamichane and the Ghale.

At that time there was a Nepali Raja at Lamjung Darbar (palace). The Lamichane went secretly to the Lamjung Raja and plotted with him against the Ghale Raja. The Lamichane minister arranged for the Ghale Raja to come unarmed to a place called Sulikot, ostensibly to make a pact of friendship with the Lamjung Raja. Beforehand, certain warriors (Lamichane?) hid their weapons in the sand at that place and when the Ghale Raja and his clansmen arrived the warriors slew them.

By one account the massacre was at Sulikot, a fortress now in ruins, near the present day village of Baglungpani, seven kilometers south east of Ghanpokhara (and only three kilometers from the Lamjung palace). By others it was at Sildhunga, a Gurung village 15 kilometers north east of Ghanpokhara, or at Sisidhunga (probably identical). According to yet another, the Ghale Raja was killed and his body tossed into the Marsiangdi River, or a tributary thereof, and his brothers fled north to Tingaun in south eastern Manang District to settle in exile. The latter version explains why some Ghale clansmen do not drink of the Marsiangdi River and/or certain of its tributaries. There are also other related folk versions of the dispute between the Lamichane and Ghale clans, and of the circumstances leading to their initial marriage alliance.

Compare the conclusion of Legend 2 to a very similar account recorded by Pignede (1962: 106-107):

LEGEND 2a

Defeat of the Ghale Raja
Alternate Version (conclusion)

... When the Lamjung king died, five men ... went to Nowokot to bring back king Kalo Sahi's son and put him on the Lamjung throne. The *ghale* king of Pojo lured the new prince into a trap and killed him. The same five men put the dead prince's brother on the throne which had again become vacant. The latter summoned the *can* (progenitors of the Lamichane) to defend him. The *can* killed the king of Pojo and drowned him in the river Marsyandi (sic). Since then, *ghale* people no longer drink water from that river. The king of Lamjung occupied the country of Pojo and gave it to the *can* who helped him govern his kingdom. Later he married a daughter of the *ghale* king. Finally, it is stated that henceforth all, *ghale, can* and others would be known as "gurung."

Pojo may be Nepalized as Pauchok and some Gurungs have identified it to me as the Pauchok village which is located in the valley of the Khudi River five kilometers southeast of Ghanpokhara and east of Ghalegaun (Ghale village). Note also that the appelation *can* (pronounced *'chan'*) converges with Lami*chane*.

All of these versions of the legend are structurally similar. They account for (1) the demise of the Ghale Raja at the hands of the Lamichane in collusion with the Nepali Raja of Lamjung, (2) the subjugation of the Gurungs under the Nepalese House of Gorkha, and (3) the initial marriage alliance between Lamichane and Ghale clans.

The answer to Lamichane clan ascendancy is implicit. The vacuum resulting from the loss of Ghale rule at the local level was filled directly by the Lamichane, i.e. by the *can*, as a gift from the Raja of Lamjung. Lamichane support for the Lamjung Raja, if true, certainly gave the House of Gorkha good reason for favoring them in local administrative appointments as headmen and later as local land revenue functionaries when the need arose.

Lamichane Officials. Administrative appointments by the House of Gorkha were of two main types in Gurung country; village headmen or chiefs, and local land revenue functionaries. In the instances of the village of Ghanpokhara and Ghaisu, both positions were granted to members of the local dominant Lamichane lineages and appear to have merely affirmed their previously established authority and power.

Originally, Gurung village headmen affirmed by the government were called *amali* or *amaldar*, derived from the Nepali term *amal* meaning "office, position . . . , honour, respect, greatness" and in military quarters having the added meaning of a non-commissioned officer of the rank of *naik* or corporal (Turner 1965: 20, 21, 337). The military connotation may indicate that the original appointees were already serving the House of Gorkha in some military capacity (alluded to in Legend 2a, above). Regmi reports that the government appointed *amali* appeared to enjoy positions equivalent to former chieftans (1963: 126-127). Later, the Gurungs dropped the Nepali terms *amali/amaldar* in favor of the Gurung *khhro* and its Nepali equivalent, *mukhya*.

The Principality of Lamjung was formally annexed by the Gorkha government in Kathmandu in 1776 A.D. Appointment of Gurung and other tribal village headmen in the hills probably dates to an earlier time when the House of Gorkha was locally powerful only in the western hills of its origin. Half a century after annexation, between 1830 and 1837 A.D., the central government instigated basic changes in its system of revenue collection throughout the hills. This involved the instalment of a second category of appointee, the local land revenue functionary called a Jimuwal or Mukhya (Regmi 1971: 72-73; 1963: 173ff.).[14] The responsibility of collecting local land taxes was commonly vested with the already recognized village headman. Thus, the Lamichane headman of such villages as Ghanpokhara and Ghaisu gained even more economic, political, and social prominence. As headmen, each presided over his village assembly and a smaller council of elders comprised of the chief (*chiba*) of each resident clan. As tax functionary, each was responsible for revenue collection from village land under production.

Succession to the combined headman-tax functionary offices quickly became hereditary, following Gurung custom. The rule of succession among Lamichane headmen is this: *the eldest son of the local dominant Lamichane lineage by a proper Char Jat endogamous marriage inherits.* If another son of the same Lamichane father is chronologically elder but is born of an illegitimate union with a Sora Jat woman, that is of a jat-exogamous union, he is commonly restricted from inheriting office. An example of the latter may be seen in Figure 1.

In large villages which incorporated several hamlets, leaders of segmented Lamichane lineages were designated as subordinate tax functionaries and as subheadmen. Ostensibly, the central government had the power to challenge and change all such local village office holders, but today's villagers can recall few instances of actual government interference. In most instances of change, they say that the local villagers instigate it and seek confirmation from higher authority. In the past, such changes occurred primarily in instances of mental incompetency, disinterest or disinclination on the part of the rightful successor, or a lack of direct patrilineal heir to the office. In every instance, however, succession to Mukhya and Jimuwal offices has remained within the dominant Lamichane clan.

The Jimuwal was not only responsible for collecting land revenues, but he could also allocate new lands as they were claimed from the forest. Apparently, he could also repossess lands abandoned by emigrating villagers (an actual instance is in the early history of Ghaisu). As headman of the village, he also had the additional authority to mediate disputes, within prescribed limits.[15] In return for his services to the government, he was allowed, as Jimuwal, to exact unpaid labor

5, 6. Gurung house-building

from the landholders under his jurisdiction, a practice called *beth* in Nepali (Regmi 1971: 102n., 107-117 *passim*) or *bid no* in Gurung. Thus, not only did he enjoy control over the allocation of the primary economic resource, the land, but he had a ready source of free manpower at his disposal, at the rate of one day's labor per household per annum.[16]

Far more important than the economic advantages they gained, the Jimuwals enjoyed a position of special privilege. They "dealt directly with the government representative at the district level and enjoyed enhanced status and authority," Regmi tells us (1971: 177). In the unique instance of Ghanpokhara's dominant Lamichane lineage, this privileged status was the stepping stone to even more authority and power as regional administrators and customs contractors called Subba. The first Gurung Subba, appointed at the turn of the twentieth century by the central government, totally eclipsed his peers and established a powerful lineage not in its fourth generation (Messerschmidt and Gurung 1974).

Notes

1. Caution is likewise advised in interpreting the figures for the northern border districts of Manang and Mustang, on Table 1. The number of Gurung speakers recorded may be higher than the actual number of ethnic Gurungs living there. It is thought that the prestige value of calling one's self "Gurung" as opposed to "Bhotia" (Tibetan) or "Lama" is the main reason for the high incidence of Gurung-speakers enumerated in those districts. Furthermore, indigenous Tibetan-speaking men may find enlistment in the Gurkha armies easier as "Gurungs."

2. For more elaborate discussions of Gurung trade, pastoralism, and agriculture, see Messerschmidt n.d., and Messerschmidt and Gurung, 1974.

3. Omitted from this categorization are small communities of Gurung migrants found in other parts of Nepal who for the most part do not use the Gurung language and who have given up other identifying cultural features.

4. Warren Glover and John Landon are linguists with the Summer Institute of Linguistics, Tribhuvan University, Kirtipur, Nepal. Warren Glover, and his wife Jessie, have established themselves as the leading experts on the Gurung language (see Glover 1969, 1971, 1972, 1974, and Glover and Glover 1972). Summer Institute specialists on the Ghale language are Larry and Marie

Seaward.
Glover and Landon have also speculated on possibly identifiable Northern and Southern Gurung dialects encompassing the Gurung speakers of eastern Manang and northern Gorkha Districts, and of southern Syangja and western Tanahu Districts, respectively. Gurungs of eastern Tanahu and southern Gorkha Districts, and in a few other locales, have forsaken their Gurung language for Nepali.

5. A more detailed discussion of Gurung social organization is found in my dissertation (Messerschmidt 1974*b*) and in the writings of Pignede (1962, 1966), Macfarlane (1972), Doherty (1974, 1975), and in the forthcoming study by Andors (n.d.).

6. Pignede comments that the jat group names "signify a difference in status, the less numerous group being of a higher status than the more numerous group, according to a formula widely known in the Gangetic plain and whose meaning is present here" (1962: 103).

7. Colloquial Gurung terms give the denotation of number only in part, although status distinctions still prevail between the two jats. Central Gurungs refer to both the Char Jat as a whole and to the Lamichane clan in particular as *khhro* 'chiefs' (*kroh* in Pignede's works.) The Lamichane clan claims predominance politically, as chiefs, among central Gurungs (although this is apparently not the case among western Gurungs observed by Pignede and Macfarlane). Among western Gurungs, the Char Jat is called *plih-gi,* 'four clans' (Pignede 1962).
The central Gurung term for the Sora Jat is *thar,* 'clans'. Among some western Gurungs, *thar* means, generally, the members of *any* clan, and is sometimes used to refer more specifically to members of the *Char* Jat (Macfarlane 1972: 43-44). Pignede refers to a similar term, *tha,* to mean men of any local lineage (1966: 189ff., 271ff.). The two terms may have a common origin. Some western Gurungs also refer to the Sora Jat as *pwaeme,* 'Tibetan' (Macfarlane 1972; N. J. Allen, personal communication). Some of Pignede's informants also used *ku-gi,* 'nine clans,' to refer to the entire Sora Jat.

8. Other legends speak of the same, or a similar, Ghale Raja residing in what is now Manang District in the ancient past (Tilman 1952: 179; Naresh Gurung, personal communication).

9. Conceivably, *plon* is related to the Tibetan *blon* meaning 'high officer of state, minister, governor.' Pignede (1962: 110-111) refers to Carrasco's

account of the *blon* as "councillors and ministers" to the chiefs of small Tibetan principalities (Carrasco 1959: 18-19).

10. The *kalas* is "a copper water pot used in the performance of religious rites (in the marriage-ceremony called *diyo kalas pujera lyauna* . . . , it is carried empty in front of the bridegroom)." The ceremony referred to is described as "a form of marriage used in castes lower than Brahmans, or between a Brahman and a woman of a lower caste" (Turner 1965: 79a, 312a).
    Ghaisu villagers know only of the use of *kalas* in marriages of non-Gurungs, i.e. between castes.

11. It would have more force if the observation stemmed from the Char Jat, rather than their allegedly inferior counterparts. Pignede's Sora Jat statement simply shifts the responsibility for the contrived account to outsiders.
    That a Brahman should propound such a model of the caste system, greatly attenuated in this instance, is a prerogative dating from the post-Vedic era (Ghurye 1950). This document also clearly places all Gurungs in a subordinate caste position beneath the 'twice-born' Brahman priest who, in the legend, expounded on Gurung origins, and the king of Kaski to whom it was told. The place of the Gurungs as fallen 'twice-born' (defiled by the prostitutes) is clearly stated. Reference to the *kalas* wedding vessel further validates their subordinate status (although whether Gurungs actually do or do not use the *kalas* is moot). Thus the Gurungs are duly accounted for in the scheme of the dominant caste society.
    It is also interesting to note that while the rule of Jat endogamy is foremost, there is allowance for hypergamous union; that is, between a lower status Sora Jat woman and a Char Jat man. This is analogous to the leniency allowed in Nepal with respect to intercaste marriage and which distinguishes the Nepali caste system from that of India in general (see Fürer-Haimendorf 1960 and Fisher 1973 for discussions of this point).

12. Neither Pignede nor I had access to the court records which may some day be found in the law archives in Kathmandu, the capital of Nepal.

13. There are several prominent and powerful Lamichane lineages at Ghanpokhara. One of them is the famous 'Subba lineage' which is described briefly in Footnote 2, Chapter 2 (page 38, below), and about which a detailed account has recently been published (Messerschmidt and Gurung 1974).

14. Originally, Mukhya meant the collector of revenue on *pakho* or unirrigated land on which maize, millet, and other dry crops are grown, and Jimuwal meant the tax collector on *khet* or irrigated land where paddy and wheat

are cultivated (Regmi 1963). The distinction between these two terms is not uniform throughout Nepal. Regmi reports that in some districts both types of revenue collectors were known only as Mukhya. In Gurung villages, on the other hand, Jimuwal came to mean land revenue collector in general, while the title of Mukhya was more closely allied to the role of headman (also called *khhro*).

15. The headman was specifically excluded from handling a clase of cases known as *pancha khat,* 'five accusations:' murder, treason, change of caste (passing), incest, and highway robbery. These offenses were referred to higher authorities for judication.

16. The Jimuwal should not be confused with the *jamindar* (sometimes *zamindar),* the 'dominant landlord,' of north India and southern Nepal, although it was very likely that he could, and in some instances did, become a dominant landlord in the hill villages.

CHAPTER TWO
The Village

Physical Setting

Ghaisu is an old settlement, nearly 2,000 meters above sea level on a ridge near the upper limits of rice agriculture.[1] Besi, a nearby hamlet, is in a valley two kilometers from Ghaisu and about one thousand meters lower. Besi was founded only 25 or 30 years ago by Gurungs of Ghaisu who wished to live near their lower fields to avoid the arduous climb daily to and from the valley. Altogether there are 131 households in Ghaisu and Besi; 123 of them are Gurung, seven are Kami caste, and one is Magar.

Ghaisu has an open assembly area on a level spot near the crest of the ridge (see Map 2). The assembly grounds are fronted by a three-sided house; both are used for large religious and social celebrations. Certain dances, dance-dreams, religious ceremonies, and weddings are held there. Public announcements are called out over the rooftops from there by a town crier, and heads of households gather on the assembly grounds to discuss village affairs and hear directives received from higher government authorities.

The assembly house is called the 'house of Durga' because of its role as the shrine to the goddess Durga during the annual festival of Dasai in the Fall. The assembly area is also occasionally given over to itinerant peddlers to display their wares.

There is a small primary school in the village. Prior to 1958, classes were taught by local ex-Gurkha soldiers. That year the central government's education plan made provision for funding permanent schools in many hill villages. Two years later a simple three-sided stone structure was built in Ghaisu with combined government and village resources. Meanwhile, the first schoolmaster, a Chhetri caste youth, was hired.

Directly in front of Ghaisu lie terraced fields descending over a thousand meters toward Besi hamlet. Behind Ghaisu the ridge drops away precipitously into a small stream where village cattle and goats are often grazed. These are communal lands. On the nearby cliffs a type of coarse grass grows which is cut for thatch

7. A highland Gurung village under snow

8. A valley village amidst corn fields

Map 2. Ghaisu Village and Besi Hamlet

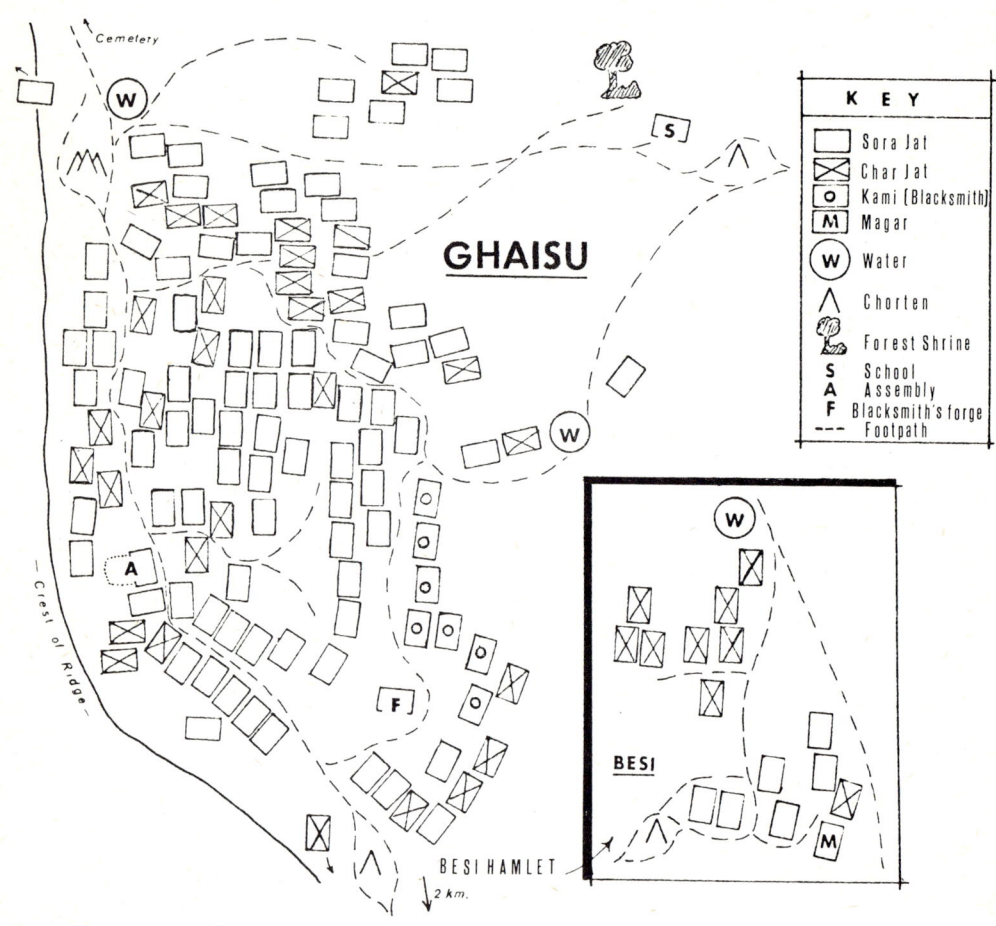

to make or repair house roofs.

On the hill above Ghaisu are several sacred sites and shrines, one of the two village springs, and the main cemetery. Well worn trails fan out and up from Ghaisu to higher pastures of the sheep and cattle and to a few unirrigated fields where upland crops are sown. Above 3,300 meters the heavily cut forest begins; it is the nearest source of wood and bamboo for fuel and building materials. Older villagers recall when the forest grew down to the village edge and wild animals preyed on livestock and devastated the crops.

Within an hour's walk north, south, and east of Ghaisu are the hamlets of Kinara, Agardi, and Talo. These settlements are bound to Ghaisu and Besi by networks of intimate social relationships, principally through marriage. They also fall within the administrative jurisdiction of Ghaisu under the government's newly designed Panchayat system.

The Outside

The wider vicinity of Ghaisu includes the large and prominent Gurung village of Ghanpokhara, several hours' walk distant, and a nearby bazaar, several villages of the Brahman and Chhetri castes, and villages of other castes and ethnic groups.

Ghanpokhara is the home of several wealthy and high status Lamichane lineages. Those of the Subba lineage, especially, are looked up to as models for aspiration, being somehow symbolic of the alleged superiority of the Lamichane clan.[2] The proximity of such outside reference groups are important in Ghaisu when considering the definition of values about status and social identity. Naresh, my principle research assistant, is the son of the last officially appointed Gurung Subba. Those who know Naresh's heritage respectfully call him 'Subba' also.

Khudi, the bazaar closest to Ghaisu, is inhabited mostly by Newari merchants who trace their origins to Kathmandu. The bazaar is very small, comprised of a few shops and inns, a post office, school, rice mill, and a medical dispensary. There is also a Hindu shrine nearby. Ghaisu villagers can purchase basic commodities at inflated prices, such as cloth of Indian and Chinese manufacture, sugar, tea, cigarettes, soap, candies, kerosene, and a variety of Ayurvedic and Western medicines. The bazaar is visited by the Gurungs en masse on the occasion of the annual Hindu festival of Magh Sakranti in mid-January, and sporadically during the year. Except for the chance meeting of Gurungs from other locales, social interaction in Khudi bazaar is of a limited economic, and sometimes religious, nature.

Nearby Brahman and Chhetri villages, and a few other ethnic and caste villages, are of relatively minor social importance to Ghaisu villagers. They seldom go to them, but Brahman and Chhetri men occasionally visit Ghaisu as moneylenders or to contract herdsmen to take their cattle to the high summer pastures, or to purchase goats, sheep, or chickens for sacrificial purposes. The Ghaisu Chhetri schoolmaster lives in one of these small villages near Khudi. In a very general way, the Brahmans also serve as a reference group to the small degree that Ghaisu villagers emulate Hindu hierarchical and religious values, but only on rare occasions are Brahman priests seen in the village.

Beyond these few outlying villages, the bazaar, and Ghanpokhara, there are several trade and administrative towns at a distance to which Ghaisu villagers occasionally travel.

The Lamjung District administrative headquarters are at Besisahar, a day's walk from Ghaisu. Besisahar is a predominantly Brahman and Newar settlement. Civil servants from Kathmandu posted there are a link between the villagers and the central government and are important communicators of new ideas.

Two day's walk south of Ghaisu is a bush airfield in Gorkha District and a new bazaar called Dumre on the Pokhara-Kathmandu road. Prior to the opening of the road in 1971 and the rapid growth of roadside bazaars as major supply depots for hillsmen, northern Lamjung Gurungs had to trek to Narayan Ghat in the Rapti Valley south of Tanahu District for supplies. That was a round trip of from eight to ten days for many. As an alternative, the villagers can trek west to Pokhara in Kaski District. Pokhara is the largest bazaar town in the western hills. It has recently acquired year-round airline service, hospitals, schools, and government offices and is the northern terminus of a new road from India, as well as the one from Kathmandu. This booming metropolis attracts many Western tourists and mountaineers. It is also a popular stopover for Gurkha soldiers on leave from the Indian and British armies and returning to Ghaisu and other hill villages. Retired soldiers visit Pokhara periodically to claim pension monies.

The only other long distance travel a Ghaisu villager might engage in is to the Gurung-Bhotia trade towns of Bhot Khola, in Manang District. They are several days' walk north, and the most compelling reason to go to them is to sell or barter rice for Tibetan salt (Messerschmidt 1972, Messerschmidt and Gurung 1974).

All travel in the hills is subject to the weather and to the demands of subsistence farming. Travel comes to an almost complete standstill during the monsoon season (June to September) when the rice must be attended and when rivers are high and bridges down, and afterwards during the time of harvest and many festivals (October and November).

Early Village History

The history of Ghaisu begins when Sora Jat men of the Yoj clan founded the hamlet of Ghai, antecedent to Ghaisu. The date of their arrival is unknown but it was probably before 1850 A.D. The eldest living villager, chief of the Yoj, a man in his 80's, remembers that during his youth (about 1900) there were only seven Yoj households in the village. Yoj clansmen say that their ancestors came from the west, from Khelo, (probably Khilang) in Kaski District.

Phle clansmen, whose origins are more obscure, lived in a nearby hamlet called Su. One tale relates that Su was depopulated by a plague and that many Phle villagers emigrated. The Yoj chief recalls that there were only two Phle households remaining in 1900. After the plague, about the turn of the century, the villagers of Ghai and the survivors of Su abandoned their respective hamlets and together founded a new village which they called Ghai-Su.

By this time it seems clear that Char Jat Lamichane clansmen had already settled in the predominantly Sora Jat hamlets of this vicinity. The Lamichane arrival is described in legend:

LEGEND 3

Early History of Ghaisu

In early times there was war between the Yoj of Ghai hamlet and the people of Syakhol, some distance away. The Yoj were weak and defenseless, continually at the mercy of the Syakhol villagers who periodically plundered Ghai and carried away the livestock. One day the elders of the Yoj clan asked an astrologer to determine the cause of their unusual suffering. He told them that because they had no Char Jat clansmen living in Ghai they were weak. Without Lamichane leadership, he said, they would continue to be defeated in battle. At that time a prominent Lamichane clansman was minister to the Ghale king of the Gurung. The astrologer advised the Yoj to kidnap the son of that Lamichane to be their leader. They could identify the Lamichane boy because he would be found sitting on a woollen blanket, whereas other boys, of lesser status, would be sitting in the dust.

"Bring the Lamichane to Ghai, raise him to manhood, invest him with leadership, and he will lead you to defeat the people of Syakhol," the astrologer advised.

Following the astrologer's advice, the Yoj clansmen travelled to Ghanpokhara (some say to Ghandrung, in distant Parbat District) and

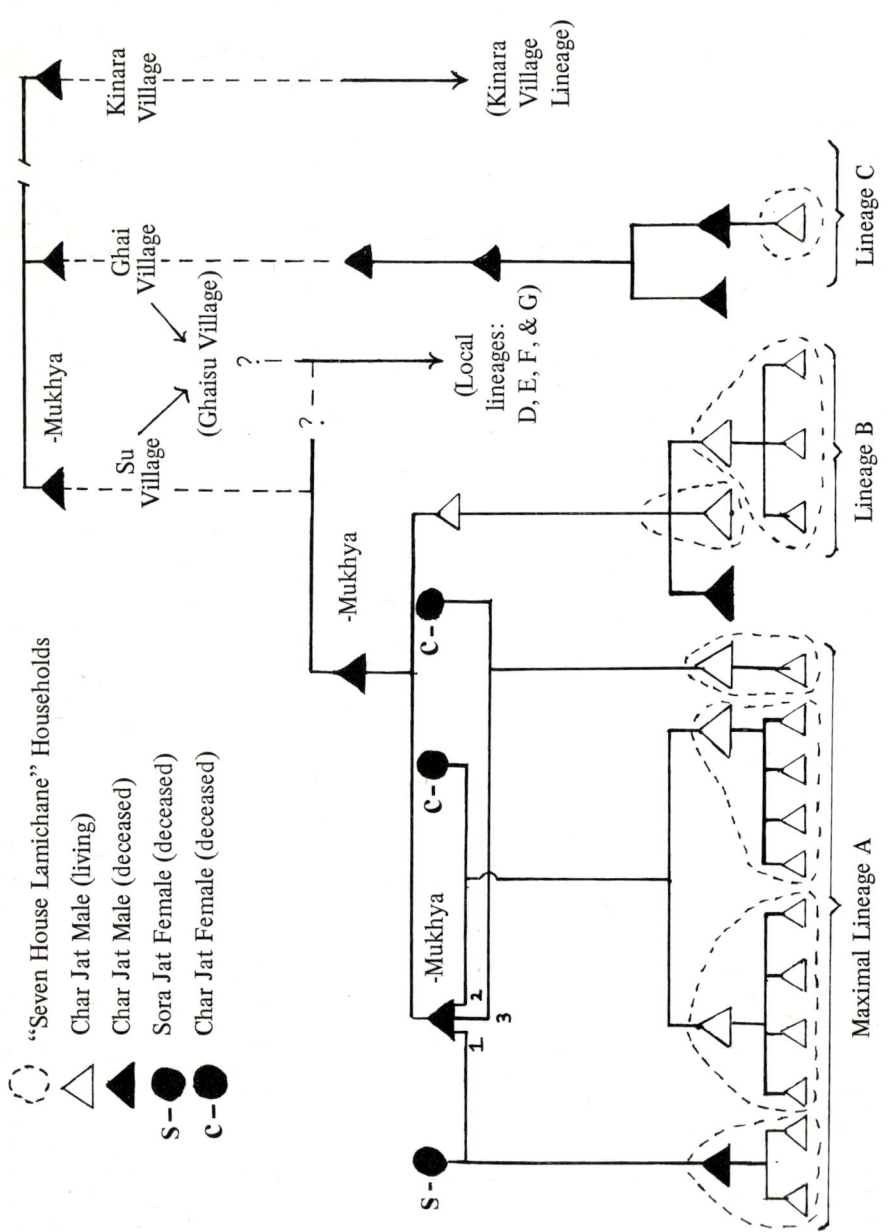

Figure 1. Lamichane Clan Genealogy, Ghaisu Village.

kidnapped the Lamichane minister's son. They raised him in Ghai and when he became of age, they gave him fields and arranged a proper marriage. Some time later the men of Ghai made a plan under his direction. They beckoned their Syakhol enemies to meet them at the river bank to make a pact of friendship (*ngyel chyab*). The men of Syakhol came unsuspecting. However, men of Ghai had hidden weapons in the sand and others hid out of sight nearby. Poisoned beer was prepared and served to the Syakhol men and when they became senseless the Yoj warriors fell on them with their weapons, slew them, and threw them into the river.[3]

After awhile the women of Syakhol sent someone to see what delayed the return of their menfolk. Hearing of the massacre, all of the widows came to that place and broke their bangles. The glass from those bangles can still be seen in the fields.

This legend is a composite of several nearly identical versions told to me by both Sora Jat and Char Jat villagers in Ghaisu. It is important in establishing the original relationship between the local Yoj and the Lamichane clans, and broadly between the jats.

Another legendary account goes on to tell how at a later time there were three Lamichane brothers who were direct descendants of the first Lamichane of Ghai. The eldest brother was the headman (Mukhya) of Ghai, the second of Su, and the youngest was headman of the nearby hamlet of Kinara. In time each brother was appointed the local land tax functionary (Jimuwal) by the ruling House of Gorkha. The jurisdiction of each was the bounds of each hamlet. When the former hamlets of Ghai and Su were abandoned and Ghaisu village was founded, the Lamichane brothers each retained their tax collectorships, and the eldest of them became the paramount head over the combined new village. The administrative division of the present Ghaisu Village Panchayat government into wards, two in Ghaisu and one in Kinara, as well as one each in the villages of Agardi and Talo, added later, are directly derived from earlier land tax jurisdictions.

In Ghaisu, Lamichane lineage A and B can be traced directly to the eldest brother, and C to the second eldest (Figure 1). These three contemporary local lineages call themselves, together, the 'Seven House (*sat ghare*) Lamichane.' Descendants of the youngest brother forming a fourth lineage are still living in Kinara, but they no longer maintain intimate ties with Ghaisu lineages.

The history of Ghaisu's Lamichane lineages D, E, F and G is more difficult to document. Some say that the ancestors of these clansmen came from villages in a nearby valley. The present (1972) village council chairman, a man of lineage D, claims descent from the original Lamichane of Ghai, but his claim is not verified.

Today in Ghaisu there are three land tax collectors, each called Jimuwal, two of whom are directly descended from the three brothers mentioned (lineages A, B, and C). The third is another man of Lamichane lineage D whose forefather was given a share of the tax collectorship of lineage A earlier this century. The exact circumstances of that division of jurisdiction are unclear. This third tax collector is the younger half-brother to the current village council chairman. The traditional rule of primogeniture in inheritance of office (page 15) does not hold in this instance, because the elder half-brother's mother was a Sora Jat women, hence her son by the Lamichane father is an impure Char Jat. As we shall see, wealth and achievement have become the important factors in favor of lineage D's local ascendancy.

Other tales of Ghaisu's settlement relate how the Nasi and other Sora Jat clans came to settle later, at the invitation of the numerically superior Yoj. The first Ghale clansmen and the first blacksmith of the Kami caste arrived only four generations ago. At that time a Yoj elder is said to have invited his fictive kinsman, a Ghale of Ghalegaun, near Ghanpokhara, to settle in Ghaisu and offered him fields to farm. As a favor, the Ghale brought with him a family of blacksmiths and established that menial caste.

It is not clear whether an affinal marriage alliance already existed between the Lamichane of Ghaisu and the Ghale of Ghalegaun, but it is known that the first Ghale took a local Lamichane woman for his second wife. Ghale lineage A descends from his first wife (clan unknown) and lineage B from the second, the Lamichane woman. Since that time, one-third of all recorded marriages of Lamichane men and Ghale men combined in Ghaisu have been with cross-cousins of the other's clan within the village. The other two-thirds are marriages to women from other nearby villages.

The most recent immigration to Ghaisu was by a household of poor Magars from southern Lamjung District. They were sponsored by and given a house in Besi under the auspices of men of Lamichane lineage D, under circumstances to be elaborated later.

Demography and Settlement Pattern

The demographic composition of the Gurungs of Ghaisu-Besi is given in Table 3 (page 33). There are 123 Gurung households. In addition, there are seven Kami blacksmith households, and one Magar.

It will be seen from the Table that the Sora Jat outnumber the Char Jat by more than two to one in total number of households (83 to 40), clans (8 to 3), and overall population (415 to 206). Among the clans, the Sora Jat Yoj, the clan of original settlers, is the largest in size (212 persons) and the Char Jat Lamichane is second (134 persons). The clans of Phle (82), Ghale (68), and Nasi (62) follow. The remaining five Sora Jat clans are represented by a single lineage apiece and constitute altogether a distinct minority of the population (59 persons altogether). Finally, there is one Lama clan family of four persons.

There appears to be little sociological significance in the positioning of residences in Ghaisu by jat of clan (see Map 2). Blacksmiths cluster near their forge hut, and the Sora Jat show some central tendancy. The Char Jat are widely scattered among the Sora Jat households.[4]

Village Economy

The contemporary Ghaisu economy is based primarily on a combination of field agriculture and mercenary soldiery, with pastoralism and trade being somewhat less important now than in the recent past (Messerschmidt 1974a). Wealth is measured in terms of production; paddy lands in the lower valley are the most productive. Salaries and pensions from soldiering with the Gurkha mercenaries away from Ghaisu are generally converted into land after the soldiers return home. As farmers, the Gurungs raise rice, maize, wheat, eleusine, millet, barley, and a few garden greens. Their fields are terraced on steep hillsides and are irrigated by diverting streams and capturing the monsoon downpours.

Early Gurung Economy. The earliest descriptions of the Gurungs are found in the published writings of Francis Buchanan (1819) and in the unpublished mid-nineteenth century notes of Brian H. Hodgson (n.d.). Both described the Gurungs as herders and traders, as well as farmers. Buchanan reports that Gurungs were avid hunters and soldiers "addicted to arms" (1819: 27, 28, 76):

> Near the Magars was settled a numerous tribe named Gurung, whose wealth chiefly consisted in sheep ... [and who] in the course of their pastoral life, ... frequent the Alpine regions in summer, and return to the vallies [sic] in winter. The men also employ themselves in weaving blankets; but they are a tribe addicted to arms ... There are ... several tribes [sic, clans] of Gurungs, such as Nisi, Bhuji, Ghali and Thagsi. The latter live nearest the snow; but all the Gurungs require a cold climate, and live much intermixed with the Bhotiyas on both sides of the snow-covered peaks of Emodus [the Himalaya, 'Emodus of the Ancients'] , and in the narrow vallies interposed, which, in the language of the country, are called Langna. The Gurungs cultivate with the hoe, and are diligent traders and miners. They convey their goods on sheep, of which they have numerous flocks .... The sheep are called Barwal and their wool is said to be

fine. It is woven into a cloth, which is finer than that of Bhotan [Tibet]. The sheep of this breed give also much milk . . .

Brian Hodgson (n.d.) describes the Gurungs as "chiefly shepherds" of yak, cow, buffalo, and large flocks of sheep:

> They dwell mostly in small villages wherein each Cot [*kothi,* 'dwelling'] is quite separate & they are adeal abroad in their goths or sheep sheds. They cultivate the ground to a considerable extent growing chiefly Makai [maize] & Kodo [eleusine, or ragee millet], making Dhero [gruel] from both & that is their favourite food. They also eat Makai dressed rice-wise & also such of their sheep as die, but they do not habitually eat their sheep. They milk them & make ghee [clarified butter] of the milk & shear & make Pankhi & Kamals [robes and blankets] of the wool; & using them also for carriage over the snows bringing back rock salt of Tibet. They are the traders across the snows, taking hence cotton & rice & wheat & Dalls [lentils] & merchants' wares also either on the sheep or on their own backs. They dwell high in the lekhs [highlands] & their [agri]culture is only Khuria [*khoriya,* 'swidden'] & Bari [dry field], chiefly the former. They are also great Shikarees [hunters] & serve much as soldiers, having been renowned for hardihood since Prithi Narain's time [18th Century]. Their Janamsthan [place of origin] is Lamjoong [sic] & there away . . .

> They dwell north of the Magars & South of the Bhotias [Tibetans] inhabiting the Lekh or mountain tops & keeping vast flocks of the Burwal sheep. East & West they stretch far but mostly Westward of Nepal proper [i.e. of Kathmandu Valley] in Lamjung, Barpate, Khelung, Lakhajeung, etc . . . They are Soldier & traders as well as shepherds; less agricultural than Magars . . . Their herds are often very large [of] 1 or 2000 sheep & their dwellings [are] on the mountain tops . . . Formerly, the Gurungs ate Cows like Bhotias; but since the Gorkha Conquest they have been staid. But all other animals nearby are licit food save the domestic pig against which they have a prejudice . . . Gurungs carry & sell salt of Tibet & are, in fact, great traders across the snows with the Bhotiahs. All the local trade & mutual wants of the immediate tribes on this & that side [of] the Himalchal, being theirs & thru them supplied.

It is said that in earlier days the Yoj clan of Ghaisu was considerably more wealthy than now, perhaps surpassing all others locally. Most of their wealth, villagers say, was in large flocks of sheep. Today those sheep herds have dwindled in size and account for very little income. The same is generally true all across the Gurung highlands.

Yoj clan landholdings in Ghaisu, said to have been vast in the past, have been subdivided over the years into ever smaller plots as the clan has expanded in number and/or as land has been lost to moneylenders and to others more powerful than they. Table 4 (page 34) which details the six most wealthy householders of Ghaisu shows only one Yoj clansman represented in 1972, the chief of the clan. This aging man inherited considerable personal wealth which he supplemented by military pension (from service in Europe with the British during World War I), by minor moneylending, and by operating petty business in his house selling items brought in from the bazaar. This Sora Jat chief is one of the most outspoken opponents of the local Char Jat who presently enjoy the most privilege, wealth, and status.

The days of dependence on shepherding and trading are long past. Contemporary wealth among Gurungs generally is based almost entirely on sedentary agricultural production and the outside income from mercenary soldiery, and from other forms of migratory wage labor.

The process of gradual ecological and cultural change in Gurung economy is very old. Today the economy reflects both long-term trends and recent changes (Messerschmidt n.d.).

Historically, the Gurungs have migrated south out of the high forested reaches at the north of their region onto the relatively lower ridges and into the river valleys of the middle hills. Ruins of early Gurung villages as high as 3,500 meters in the forest of Lamjung Himal, for example, attest to their early habitation there (*ibid.*). Today, the bounds of Gurung habitation are from 2,500 meters down to approximately 1,000 meters in elevation. Some of the villages at the upper limits of this range show signs of continuing down migration. The village of Ghanpokhara, for example, set on a ridge at 2,500 meters, has become a virtual ghost village over the past generation. Farmers from Ghanpokhara have dispersed permanently into the fertile valleys below, along the Khudi and Modi Rivers, displacing, in some instances, earlier settlers. The recent founding of Besi as a satellite hamlet of Ghaisu, in the lower valley, is a similar although much smaller example of down migration.

Recent Trends. A number of factors have changed the complexion of Gurung economy in recent decades. As the Gurungs migrated to lower and more southerly locations, they turned toward field agriculture and to raising paddy, corn, and other grains. Furthermore, with the increased demand to feed a steadily rising population, many lower forest lands, once marginal, have been reclaimed and put to the plow (see Macfarlane 1972 and Messerschmidt n.d.). The situation has caused a loss in the amount of pasture land available for keeping sheep and cattle at lower elevations in winter. Shepherding has declined as a direct result of these and other factors, such as the reported decimation of herds by epidemic and plague (Pignede 1966: 135; Tod Ragsdale and J.N.B. Shrestha, personal communications, 1974). Coupled with the availability of cheap textiles from

Indian sources, the traditional home manufacture and the sale or trade of Gurung-made woollens has been curtailed, and in some villages is almost totally non-existent (Macfarlane 1972). Gurung blankets and robes, once important trade items, are now luxury items, so scarce and priced so high that only wealthy lowlanders, merchants, and city dwellers, and an occasional tourist, can afford to buy them in the markets of Kathmandu and Pokhara.

Transhimalayan trade has declined for other reasons. The increased availability of Indian salt at competitive prices beginning earlier this century has made the arduous trip to the Tibetan border regions for rock salt unrewarding (see Fürer-Haimendorf 1974/1975 for discussions of this trend). Only villagers living close to the northern trade routes and far from the sources of Indian salt continue to trek north to the trade marts of Thonje, Bagarchap, and Chame in Bhot Khola. During the 1950's, the Tibetan salt for Nepalese grain and commodities trade was brought to a virtual standstill when the Chinese authorities in Tibet closed the border (Messerschmidt and Gurung 1974). The Tibetan trade has not yet been fully re-established and the easily accessible Indian salt and commodities has diverted the hillsmen southward.

Given these various contingencies and the steadily growing view that the land itself is becoming a scarce resource, many Gurung villagers have turned to various forms of migratory wage labor to support themselves. Wage labor in this instance is mainly mercenary soldiery in the British and Indian armies, and voluntary enlistment in the Royal Nepal Army. It also includes, to a lesser extent, work in the cities of north India and in Kathmandu, and portering and field work for wealthy merchants and landowners in the lower valleys.

Other sources of cash income are minor in comparison to soldiery. They include such small enterprises as the sale of clarified butter from the cattle and water buffalo herds, the occasional sale of livestock (sheep, goats, cattle, buffalo, chickens), and the sale of bamboo wicker basketry, homespun woollen blankets and robes mentioned earlier, and hempen cloth. Two or three men in Ghaisu, all ex-soldiers, sell small quantities of cigarettes, kerosene, mustard oil, cloth, matches, sugar, and other oddments in their homes. There is some wage labor (*nimek*) available within the village, usually paid for in grain or applied as credit against personal debts. Share-cropping (*adhiya*, 'halves') and cooperative work parties (*nogar, parma, guhar*) are also common. Nogar, the principle form of cooperative labor, is described later.

Rotating credit associations (*dhikur*), although apparently popular in Ghaisu in the past, are non-existent today; only one Ghaisu villager presently participates in a very small credit association of a neighboring village. Rotating credit seems

9, 10. Gurung men slaughtering a water buffalo for a feast

never to have been as important here as elsewhere among the neighboring Thakali and other ethnic groups (Messerschmidt 1972, 1973; Hitchcock n.d.; Doherty n.d.). Above all, soldiery is the primary source of working capital. Along with landed inheritance, it is a main factor to be considered in any discussion of the contemporary distribution of wealth and status in Ghaisu.

Contemporary Ghaisu Economy. When a Ghaisu villager speaks of wealth, he talks in terms of landholdings of a particular household, calculating grain yield, primarily rice, in a typical year. Hence, wealth in local parlance is landed wealth. Agricultural land can be acquired by several means: through inheritance, by holding power over registration and allocation of land (as the tax collector does), and by reclamation of land from the forest (which is subject to tax registration). Recently, since cash has become a common form of exchange in the hills, land is being acquired by outright purchase, or indirectly through repayment of debts in moneylending. The most desirable and productive land is irrigated paddy land, usually in the valley bottoms.

In Ghaisu today, a minority of Char Jat households dominate the landed wealth, as well as soldiery. Among them, the Lamichane clan is proportionately richer relative to its size than any other clan (see Tables 4, 5, and 6 below). The Char Jat account for only 40 households in the village; that is, about 33 per cent of the total 123 Gurung households. The Sora Jat account for 83 households of 67 per cent. Looking at Table 5, however, one sees that among the 26 wealthiest households (representing 21 per cent of the village) a disproportionate 18 are Char Jat, 15 of which are Lamichane, while only eight are Sora Jat. Considering all households in which at least one soldier is resident, 23 (19 per cent) are Char Jat, 14 of which are Lamichane, compared with only 41 Sora Jat soldier households (33 per cent).

Table 6 shows percentages of agricultural production compared with percentage of households by clan and jat in Ghaisu. The Lamichane maintain a striking dominance in field grain production. Although they represent only 21 percent of the households, the Lamichane control 48 per cent of the rice crop and 32 per cent of all other major crops (maize, wheat, barley, eleusine, millet, and soybean), altogether 40 per cent of the entire yield of the village. Considering the three local Char Jat clans combined, the Char Jat control almost half (48 per cent) of the total village annual grain harvest, yet they account for only 33 per cent of the households. The Sora Jat, with a majority of 66 per cent of the households, control only 52 per cent of the total harvest. It should be noted, however, that share-cropping and wage labor ameliorate the imbalance between the jats to some degree. Some poorer villagers, mostly Sora Jat, have access to crops harvested on wealthier (mostly Char Jat) villagers' lands. Nonetheless, in an economy operating

Table 3 Demography of Ghaisu Village (1972); Gurung.

Jat & Clan		Local Lineage	Number of Households	Number of Persons
Char Jat				
Lamichane		A	4	25
		B	2	9
		C	1	5
		D	7	41
		E	2	8
		F	4	20
		G	6	26
		7	26	134
Ghale		A	4	28
		B	9	40
		2	13	68
Lama*		A	1	4
		1	1	4
Totals:	3	10	40	206
Sora Jat				
Yoj		A	4	22
		B	20	100
		C	9	54
		D	2	9
		E	6	27
		5	41	212
Phle		A	11	47
		B	5	19
		C	4	16
		3	20	82
Nasi		A	6	28
		B	5	28
		C	1	6
		3	12	62
Ngor		A	3	14
Thorche		A	3	16
Pajyu		A	2	15
Tu		A	1	8
Kromche		A	1	6
		5	10	59
Totals:	8	16	83	415
Grand Totals:	11	26	123	621

*The Lama clan is represented by one household; its presence will be understood throughout the dissertation, although infrequently mentioned.

Table 4. The Six Wealthiest Householders, Ghaisu (1972)*

Char Jat

Half-Brothers {
1. Lamichane Lineage A -

    Pensioned ex-soldier; one son currently in army.
    Minor moneylender.

2. Lamichane Lineage A -

    Former Mukhya; Jimuwal; clan chief.
    Pensioned ex-soldier; three sons currently in army.
    Minor moneylender.
}

3. Lamichane Lineage C -

    Jimuwal.
    Son of pensioned ex-soldier (recently deceased).
    Minor moneylender.

Half-Brothers {
4. Lamichane Lineage D -

    Jimuwal.
    Non-soldier.
    Minor moneylender.

5. Lamichane Lineage D -

    Village council chairman.
    Non-soldier.
    Major moneylender.
}

Sora Jat

6. Yoj Lineage A -

    Clan chief.
    Non-pensioned ex-soldier; one adopted son (Thorche clan) who is a pensioned ex-soldier; one grandson (Thorche) who is currently in army.
    Petty village merchant.
    Minor moneylender.

---

*Number 1 is exceptionally wealthy by village standards. Numbers 2 through 6 rank about equal with each other but are less wealthy than Number 1. Wealth is based on landholdings calculated from total grain yield by household in an average year. The primary crop of each of these wealthy householders is paddy.

Table 5. Soldiers Among the 26 Wealthiest Households, Ghaisu (1972).

Jat & Clan	Soldier Households			Non-soldier Households	All Households
	Pension	No Pension	Total		
Char Jat					
Lamichane	6	2	8	7	15
Ghale	3	-	3	-	3
Totals:	9	2	11	7	18
Sora Jat					
Yoj	2	3	5	2	7
Nasi	-	-	-	1	1
Totals:	2	3	5	3	8
Grand Totals:	11	5	16	10	26

Table 6. Grain Production by Clan & Jat, Ghaisu (1972).

Jat & Clan	% Households	% Crop		% Total Harvest
		Rice	Other	
Char Jat				
Lamichane	21	48	32	40
All Other Clans	12	10	8	8
Totals:	33	58	40	48
Sora Jat				
Yoj	33	22	30	26
All Other Clans	33	20	30	26
Totals:	66	42	60	52
Grand Totals:	100%	100%	100%	100%

at subsistence level, the disparity between the jats shown by these tables is indicative of hardship among the Sora Jat.

Soldiery is directly related to landed wealth; pensions and salaries are regularly invested in land. In Ghaisu, 16 (62 per cent) of the 26 wealthiest households are soldier households. Of them, the largest number are Char Jat. Furthermore, in looking at Char Jat soldier households alone, 11 of the 23 are among the wealthiest households of the village; eight of those are Lamichane.

The monetary advantages of soldiery are significant. They are discussed at length by both Pignede (1966) for Mohoriya village in Parbat District (as of 1958) and by Macfarlane (1972) for Thak village in Kaski District (as of 1969). Soldiery in those villages and in Ghaisu has held almost equal importance,[5] but the data on Thak are the most reliably comparable with Ghaisu in 1972.

Macfarlane reports (1972: 328-336) that the amount of salary and retirement pay that a soldier can expect to receive depends on such variables as length of service, rank, and service-related disabilities. Nonetheless, certain generalities are clear. A rifleman coming home from British service in Malaysia would bring with him an estimated Rs. 3,000 after three years of service, while a man of higher rank might accumulate as much as Rs. 5,000. The figures from Indian Army service are Rs. 1,000 and Rs. 2,000, respectively. Officers with an even longer service record would accumulate much larger sums. (Exchange rates at the time under discussion were approximately Rs. 10 to U.S. $ 1.00.)

Some of the soldiers' salaries and pensions go toward buying goods such as radios, watches, clothing, and gold; but most cash from soldiering is invested in land, either by direct purchase or through the intermediary step of lending money which is eventually repaid in land. The brief life history information given in Table 4 indicates the important relationship of soldiery to wealth. With only the exceptions of the two brothers of Lamichane lineage D (numbers 4 and 5 on the Table) soldiery is a dominant characteristic in the life of the wealthiest few.

Wealth and soldiery work together in another way. The already wealthy householders, primarily the Char Jat, can best afford to send sons or brothers off to military service in return for which they further enhance family fortune in the long term. The men of poorer households, generally of the Sora Jat, are bound to stay on the land by their indebtedness and the continual pressures to make ends meet. Only a few of the poorer young men, generally from large families, take advantage of the military option, often driven to it by economic desparation. Relatively few soldiers among the poorer Sora Jat tend to stay as long in service as the wealthier Char Jat soldiers. Compare the number of pensioners on Table 5 above. At home, the poor either work on their own meager land holdings (and every household claims some measure of land, however small) and/or they work as share-croppers or as wage laborers on the lands of wealthier households.

Interestingly, Macfarlane found quite the opposite situation regarding soldiery and wealth in the village of Thak. His data show that instead of the wealthy Char Jat households, "it is the medium-poor Gurung households . . . who have most access to army funds." These were predominantly Sora Jat households which had "insufficient lands on which to live in the village. The flow of cash from outside helps to balance them against the wealthier households which have had less incentive to send their sons away from the village" (1972: 335).

Ghaisu data show, however, that the wealth of a household is not the main criterion in determining incentive, or lack of it, to join the military. Different circumstances between the Char Jat of Thak and those of Ghaisu, particularly in the development of local economic and political power and status, must also be taken into account. In Thak, the Char Jat were original settlers. They controlled the land and were apparently always much better off (until recently) than the Sora Jat (*ibid.*). In Ghaisu, however, a somewhat different situation has occurred. There the Sora Jat were first settlers and they, not the Char Jat, originally controlled local land resources and, until the arrival of the Lamichane, the local power, both political and economic. Consequently, the Char Jat in Ghaisu have had to work at improving their position. They have long sought to elevate their economic status to match it with their traditional political power as headmen and their jat's higher social status. They have successfully done this by several means. As Jimuwals they acquired power over land resources through the means of land registration and tax collection as well as the free labor due to them in return. Coupled with their traditional roles as Mukhya, or headmen, they alone possessed the tools necessary to enhance wealth and social status simultaneously. Soldiery was viewed simply as another way to accelerate economic ascendancy and in the end it has allowed them to virtually eclipse the Sora Jat altogether. The local Ghale clan has benefited mainly from an affinal relationship through marriage with the Lamichane, as well as by an equally active pursuit of military service.

Notes

1. Ghaisu is a pseudonym, to maintain the anonymity promised to the villagers. Besi is also a fictitious name, as well as Kinara, Agardi, and Talo which are discussed below. All other place names, including Ghanpokhara, are correct, and all places indicated on Map 1 are accurately placed.

2. As a group the dominant lineage of Upper Ghanpokhara village, the so-called Lamichane Subbas, stand out. Beginning at the first of this century, men of that lineage controlled all commerce along the upper Marsiangdi River trade route through Lamjung and the region of Bhot Khola, in Manang District, to the Tibetan border. They held the government revenue contracts (now discontinued) and certain powers as magistrates. In time, they acquired the regional administrative office and hereditary title of 'Subba' in the neighboring border region of Thak Khola, in Mustang District, and in the Terai region along the Indian border. This privileged position, combined with the hereditary roles of Jimuwal and Mukhya locally in northern Lamjung and in the Tibetan border districts of Manang and northern Gorkha, gave the Subbas tremendous economic and political advantage and social prestige throughout the entire central Gurung country (Messerschmidt and Gurung 1974).

3. Note the similarity between this episode and that of the murder of the Ghale king by the Raja of Lamjung in Legend 2a.

4. In villages which other researchers have studied there appears to be more distinct residential clustering by jat (Pignede 1966: 64; Macfarlane 1972: 40).

5. Soldiers accounted for approximately 16 per cent of the total population of Ghaisu in 1972, 17 per cent of the population of Thak in 1969, and 19 per cent of the population of Mohoriya in 1958 (Macfarlane 1972: 328-336; Pignede 1966: 54-57).

CHAPTER THREE
Interaction Groups and Marriage

The Local Lineage. Jat membership and status are important in considering group interaction in Ghaisu, but before describing this, I must introduce the reader to the importance of that component of the jat called a local lineage. Certain aspects of one's individual social identity are more closely tied within the village to a particular local lineage than to any other social unit.

Another student of Gurung society, Alan Macfarlane, has characterized Gurung social structure as "very fluid," one in which kinship units larger than the family (i.e. lineage, clan) "are not of great importance" (1972: 27-28). In my dissertation I have argued that "in Ghaisu . . . the social structure can be characterized only as [comparatively] tight," one in which close allegiance to lineage is critically important (1974b:58-59). Since writing that, Macfarlane has questioned the dichotomy and in retrospect, I can only agree with him that in general, Gurung society appears quite fluid and flexible. In contrast to the rigid caste system of South Asia, for example, the Gurung system is a model of flexibility. I suspect that our different perspectives stem in part from quite different social and cultural circumstances in the village we studied. Thak is described by Macfarlane as a village approaching serious overpopulation, a village with an extremely limited natural resource base (e.g. land for tilling and grazing, wood for burning and building, et cetera), and one in which considerable change from earlier, traditional Gurung cultural patterns has been experienced. Ghaisu society, on the other hand, is quite traditional, and the villagers pride themselves on retaining what they perceive to be older cultural and social patterns. They have so far had to contend with relatively few changes imposed from outside, and my data show that what changes they have endured recently have not been well received overall. In Ghaisu, the lineage and the clan are the loci of significant social interaction and cohesion, and form the bases of corporate work, play, and ritual attentions.[1] In Thak, apparently, the trend is toward a strong identity based on the family unit at the expense of the lineage and clan. One may argue that the day is not far off when Ghaisu's traditionalism will change, perhaps must change, if the villagers are to accommodate to the modernity that is affecting much of the rest of Nepal. At such time, perhaps, we will see a decline in the importance of lineage and a greater focus on the family as the primary social unit. To some degree, such changes may be foreshadowed in the data on conflict and change elucidated in this study.

At the local lineage level, the responsibilities, obligations, and rights of an individual Gurung as both kinsman and affine are most intense. The local lineage and subdivisions within it are of paramount importance at times of life crises (particularly marriage and death), for inheritance, in religious ritual obligations, in relation to certain administrative privileges, and in cooperative alliances and the bonds of fictive kinship.

In village level interaction, particularly in cooperative endeavours and alliance relationships, individual behaviour and the structure of groups are greatly influenced by one's lineage membership. To a significant degree the lineage is expected to support its individual members in confrontations with persons of other lineages, clans, and jats. Generally speaking, however, the local lineage has no relevance to outsiders except as they are related by marriage.

For certain purposes further segmentation into sub-lineages occurs; this relates to the nature and degree of interpersonal relationships and regulates specific rights, obligations, and duties between those involved. The sub-lineage stands midway between the nuclear family and the local lineage. In instances where a clan or local lineage is exceedingly small, as is often the case in villages the size of Ghaisu, the criteria for differentiating sub-lineages may become blurred. Not uncommonly, too, lineage and clan merge as one and the same unit. Where a lineage is large and cumbersome in terms of population and geographic dispersion, as at Ghanpokhara, sub-lineages gain practical importance and identification with clan may take on less significance.

The men of the local lineage are called *tha-mai,* 'primary patrilineal descent group.' Fellow clansmen, so-called by members of the clan, are *bhai-mai,* 'brothers.' One may also speak of 'jat brothers' and of 'fictive bond brothers,' Some local clans are so small in Ghaisu that they comprise a single lineage. The clans and lineages of Ghaisu are listed in Table 3, page 33, with size of membership and number of households.

Fictive Kinship. Fictive kinship rounds out many economic and political relationships between fellow Gurungs, and between Gurungs and non-Gurungs. Fictive kinship is called *mit lagaunu* in Nepali and *ngyel chyab* in Gurung, literally 'to take a bond brother.' Gurung men who are in such bond brother relationships to each other are called *mit* or *ngyela* (sometimes *ngyeloh*); fictive sisters are *mitini* or *ngyelsyo* to each other. Gurung fictive kin nomenclature extends outwards from one's bond brother to his wife, mother, father, son, daughter, and so forth, eventually encompassing lineage, clan, and jat brothers *(ngyel bhai-mai)* in a generalized bond relationship. Both the specific bonds between individuals and the general bonds between corporate kin groups have significance in social interaction as is illustrated in Figure 2.[2]

The raison d'etre of fictive kinship among the Gurungs is mutual affection and mutual aid. Occasionally bond brotherhood relationships are used to seal a pack or treaty between hostile parties as exemplified in Legend 3. One makes a bond relationship with a person of his own sex and generation and of the opposite jat. Outside of Gurung society, the existence of fictive kin bonds between two individuals precludes marriage between members of their respective descent groups or castes, say for example, between Brahman and Chhetri castes which frequently intermarry in Nepali society. Within the Gurung tribe, however, the extensive of the rule of jat endogamy already precludes marriage between persons of the same descent group.

Bond brothers often share ties of commonality; for example, they may have grown up, gone to school, traded, travelled, and/or served in military service together. The bond relationship may be established, in fact, to enhance one or another of these ties (see Hitchcock n.d. on Magar *mit* for trading purposes).

Either party may initiate the relationship. Elaborate ritual such as that described for Nepali *mit* by Okada (1957) is uncommon for Gurung *ngyel*.

Figure 2. Fictive Kinship Bonds in Ghaisu.

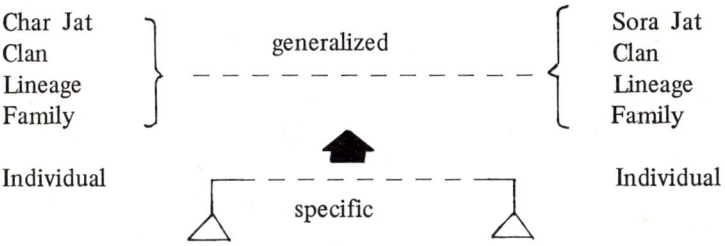

Two Gurung friends who wish to initiate a fictive kin bond simply call a few close friends and relatives together to witness the formal pact and share a small feast. An astrologer may be asked to select an auspicious day and a lama or shaman may be present to give his blessing, but neither of these ritualists is essential. The two initiates join arms and give each other *tika* (or *ashik*), a daub of rice on the forehead as a blessing to solemnize the occasion. Thereafter, other persons present may give them each small gifts of a rupee or two and a white turban cloth (*kregi*). Thenceforth, the two individuals are pledged in mutual respect and friendship, to aid each other in times of crisis or need, and to act toward one another as if real brothers.

Unformalized fictive kin bonds are also recognized and are called *ngyel su,* 'mouth bond,' or what we might call informal fictive kinship. In the mouth bond relationship, two close friends might off-handedly refer to each other as *ngyela* and may even observe some of the obligations required of true bond brothers. My wife and I were frequently called *ngyela* and *ngyelsyo* by men and women who considered themselves, and we them, as close friends.

Sometimes very old and originally true bonds, maintained only on a very generalized level, and about which specific details are obscure or long forgotten, are also called mouth bond. Over time they tend to lose their original function to the groups involved and may evolve into cooperative friendships such as *pate bhai-mai* which is reserved for mutual aid on specific, usually feasting, occasions.

Certain obligations between true bond brothers are important. Their neglect by either party is considered an offense by the other and may eventually lead to severing the relationship. Thus, by neglect of *ngyel* obligations they can be manipulated to promote larger ends. The obligations are these: One's bond brother is always invited personally to attend the major life crises ceremonies of one's self, family, and lineage. The bond brother is expected, furthermore, to come bringing gifts of *kregi kramo;* literally, he presents a white turban cloth (*kregi*) to a man and a coloured shawl (*kramo*) to a woman being honored by the occasion. He also presents them with a few token rupees. At weddings of one's sisters or daughters, the bond brother washes the girls' feet as if they were member of his own patrilineage. At one's death, or the death of an immediate kin, a parent, sibling, spouse, or child, the bond brother observes mourning and a mild death pollution. In the instance of the death of a more distant kinsman, the obligations are attenuated and the bond brother may pay only brief or token attention to them. As indicated, mutual obligations between specific bond brothers extend outward to include each other's descent groups, but at the group level obligations become generalized and are not rigidly observed.

It is at the generalized level that Gurung *ngyel* and Nepalese *mit* institutions are most clearly different from each other. The *mit* relationship is recognized to extend to a mit's closest relatives only in terms of the rules of avoidance, marriage, and kinship nomenclature. Beyond that, obligations between respective descent groups or castes are not usually recognized (Okada 1957). Among the Gurung, however, such broadly reciprocal obligations are very important and the two clans or jats involved are expected to be represented at time of major life crises of the reciprocal bond kinsmen. In the context of a funeral, for example, it is expected that the Gurung clansmen sponsoring the ceremonies will personally invite certain clansmen of the opposite jat with whom they recognize a generalized bond relationship. Participation in the final feast of the commemorative funerary celebrations is particularly important. Neglect of these responsibilities is a serious insult.

In conclusion, the essential difference between Nepalese *mit* and Gurung *ngyel* is in the nature of obligations. Their broad extension in Gurung society reflects the egalitarian nature of tribal society. It is one of the most likely institutions to demonstrate Gurung solidarity and unity, by its linking of individuals, lineages, and clans of the opposite jats. Should a Nepalese man's bond brother be of a lower caste, his presence at the man's rite of passage ceremonies would be inappropriate, perhaps defiling. Among the Gurungs, however, his presence is expected and proper.

Youth Associations. Significant socialization and interaction, particularly in terms of preparation for marriage and in encouraging the harmonious functioning of everyday village life, are fostered in Gurung youth associations called *rodi*.[3] A rodi is an association of young people who work and have fun together. There may be several rodi groups in a village, each of which is organized around a neighborhood dormitory. Boys and girls gather at the rodi houses in the evenings for entertainment, mostly dancing and singing, while during the daytime they may form the nuclei of organized field work parties.

The Gurungs make the distinction between the institution of rodi (*rodi laba*, 'to do *rodi*') and its setting, the rodi house (*rodi ti* or *rodi ghar*). This distinction is also apparent in the brief literature on Gurung rodi. Pignede defines rodi as the custom of evening meetings among the young, popular with the Gurungs (1966: 217) and Bista calls it a "club for boys and girls . . ." (1967: 78). It is also described as a "young people's meeting house" or "communal house" (Macfarlane 1972: 55, 117; Pignede 1966: 260). Andors (1974) describes rodi as "a nightly social gathering place, a semi-permanent dormitory where young girls and boys of the village congregate to sing, talk and joke." She shows disdain for the tendancy to view rodi as a sort of "social 'night-club'," then demonstrates the integral part it plays in the economic, social, and ritual organisation of village life.[4, 5]

Membership in rodi is determined by age and sex. Rodi is essentially a girl's institution to which boys are invited. Each evening the girls retire to their dormitory where they entertain and are entertained by visiting boys, and where they sleep. The group of boys, although sometimes referred to as 'boys' rodi' (*maie-mai rodi*), are loosely organized at best and have neither specific names nor a dormitory house of their own (cf. Andors 1974). My discussion centers on 'girls' rodi' (*ri-mai rodi*) of Ghaisu, each of which is organized around a sponsoring adult whose own house becomes the dormitory and by whose name that rodi is identified (e.g. 'Ram Lal's rodi'). Sponsors are usually middle aged couples who have a daughter of participating age. As the head of the rodi house, the male sponsor is called 'rodi father' (*rodi ab* or *ro ab*) and his wife is the 'rodi mother' (*rodi am*). Members call themselves, collectively, 'rodi friends' (*rodir-bai ri-mai*). There are no other named categories of persons or special offices in the rodis of Ghaisu. The associations are quite egalitarian, although it is natural for older and more mature girls to oversee and sometimes dominate certain activities and relationships within the groups, particularly when visiting boys are involved.

Girls first join rodi at about the age of eight or nine, and may participate until their mid-twenties, by which time they are usually married. Active participation usually drops off after marriage and almost certainly after a young wife has borne her first child.

There are two categories of rodi, differentiated by age.[6] A young girl *(kolo)* joins a *kol-mai* rodi for girls roughly between the ages of eight and thirteen. A girl older than that (*theba*), up to age 22 or 23 joins a *theb-mai* rodi.[7] Normally, Rodi may involve anywhere from 10 to 15 girls from a number of clans and both jats (although this flexibility has changed radically since 1970 to conform with jat boundaries; that is, rodi has become jat-endogamous.)

Membership is not compulsory, but peer group pressure to join is strong where rodi is considered to be an important or approved social institution. A girl may either ask or be asked to join a particular rodi group. There is no formal initiation rite upon joining, but at the wedding of a rodi girl a 'separation meal' (*phre kai*) is eaten by the group, and one or several of the bride's close girl friends are selected to be her attendants (*samsyo*). These friends will stay with her during the initial few days of her married life until the rite of *khi chub* is celebrated. As a member of a rodi, each girl is expected to participate in and support the various group activities equally with her associates. At times, each girl's parents, particularly her father, give material and financial assistance and chaperone her and her friends on trips to visit boys in neighboring villages, or on longer treks to distant fairs, festivals, and pilgrimage sites.

A rodi disbands naturally when all or most of its members stop participating actively. A girl who marries out of her home village ceases participation upon taking up permanent residence with her spouse. This occurs sometimes several years after marriage and often corresponds to the birth of the first child. Girls who marry near home may continue active membership for many years.

Older men are sometimes seen in rodi parties. They are usually men whose first marriages have not worked out and who are looking for entertainment and possibly for a second wife. Macfarlane notes that when rodi was active in Thak village "married women often attended, especially when their husbands were away in the army; they [rodis] were, in fact, a useful method of dealing with the male absence after marriage" (1972: 56). No older women were observed attending rodis in Ghaisu although the incidence of soldiery is virtually identical to that of Thak village.

The main functions of rodi are recreation and pre-marital socialization, which aids the smooth transition of youth to adulthood and enhances the efficient functioning of village life. They entertain each other in the evenings and long into the nights with dancing, drumming, singing, and joking. Gifts are exchanged reciprocally, symbolizing close interpersonal ties of affection. Boys give the girls hand made bamboo cigarette holders and combs, and the girls give colourful crocheted handkerchiefs to the boys.

Amorous adventures clearly result from these interactions. As one young man so tactfully said it, "rodi helps boys and girls to understand each others' natures." Another villager, a rodi father, said that rodi is, after all, the place for a girl to "have fun" and to gain experience prior to marriage. One old woman was more direct: "in rodi a girl finds affection, love (*maya*)."[8]

Ideally, cross-cousin marriage directs amorous choice. Boys and girls of the same clan are considered to be 'brothers and sisters' and practice avoidance. The basic rule of jat endogamy should prohibit Char Jat/Sora Jat affairs. But, as is so often the case, social fact does not always equate with the ideal. The Gurungs recognize that amorous adventures in rodi lead to marriage by elopement, an alternative to formal arrangements. At the same time, overt sexual relations or pregnancy resulting from premarital adventures are frowned upon. It is not the case, however, that the children born of liaisons in rodi are deprived of social status (as Srivastava [1953] reports for Rang-Bang youth associations in north India), unless, of course, the relationship is incestuous.

A no less important function of rodi is its role as the nucleus of a type of cooperative agricultural work party called *nogar.* By its nature, a nogar is a temporary association, organized seasonally to perform such tasks as preparing fields, sowing millet, maize, and eleusine grain, transplanting paddy, weeding, and harvesting.[9] Membership numbers from 10 to 20 or more persons, mostly young, who are occasionally joined by adults. Usually the girls of a rodi will invite a number of boys to join with them in forming a nogar party for a particular task. One such group of members stays together only for as many days as there are participants, working successively in the fields of each member's family. In this way, the nogar party accomplishes in one day what a single farmer would take many to finish.

Pignede (1966: 127-129) was impressed with "l'esprit du *nogar*," one of cooperative reciprocity, good fun, and camaraderie. Members laugh and sing in the fields as they work, stopping only for a mid-afternoon lunch supplied by the host of the day. After the last day of work they join together in a feast (*nogar syo kai*) to which each contributes rice, butter, and money to purchase a goat or chicken. The institution of nogar is found throughout Gurung country with minor variations from one locale to the next. Recent changes in Ghaisu nogars mirror a realignment in rodi membership.

Closely associated with rodi is a troupe of village youth who stage popular Nepali dances and short skits at festivals and during the holidays of the winter season. Their performances, called *tetar* (*tetar laba*, 'theatre doing') are described by one observer as "a mixture of dancing, singing and comedy" (Macfarlane 1972: 58; see also Andors 1974). Membership is comprised of boys and girls who associate in rodi. They are directed by a rodi father or some other talented or interested person.

By tradition, Ghaisu's entire populace has always supported one mixed-jat tetar troupe, but in 1970 a second group was formed to facilitate a realignment in membership by strict jat allegiance with similar changes in rodi and nogar groupings.

Rodi is also important in several socio-religious activities. When Gurung villagers, young and old, go on long pilgrimages to distant holy shrines, fairs, or festivals (*jatra*) they are often the members, chaperones, or guests of a particular rodi. Twice a year such travelling (*jatra yaba*) is undertaken on the Hindu holy days of Magh Sakranti and Janai Purnima. The former falls on the first day of the month of Magh (mid-January to mid-February) when regional and village fairs are scheduled in the lower valleys to coincide in time and place with Hindu religious celebrations. Some rodi groups go at this time as far as a holy site near Narayan Ghat south of Tanahu District or to Pokhara in the west.

The festival of Janai Purnima is observed on the full moon day of July or August. On this day, Hindu pilgrims of the castes and ehtnic groups trek to sacred 'milk lakes' (*dudh pokhari*) as high as 4,500 meters to bathe, worship, and receive spiritual renewal. Because these trips may be long and arduous, the rodi girls will invite several young men whom they call 'guide boys' (*nari maie-mai*) to accompany them. Rather elaborate tradition attends the departure and return of the group at the village, during the daily events of the trek, and for the ritual activities at their destination.

As usual, light-hearted fun and reciprocity prevail. The girls donate and prepare the food for the entire journey, while the boys reciprocate as load carriers and by giving gifts of money and ritualized expressions of respect and gratitude.

Finally, rodi girls participate as a group in the religious conjunction with a loosely organized committee of village boys for *ghanto,* a performance of dance and drama. Ghanto is described in detail later in the book.

Elsewhere in Gurung society great changes between contemporary and traditional rodi associations, even in some instances its abolishment, have been noted. Notions about the wider significance of rodi are being re-evaluated where contact with the Nepalese caste system is intimate, as between Gurungs and Brahman-Chhetris in the lower valleys. There, custom tends toward emulation of the dominant Hindu caste values. In such instances, rodi has taken on negative value. Pignede and Macfarlane lived and studied in reform minded villages where rodi was considered to be a bad influence on the young people and morally degrading in the eyes of the dominant group, the neighboring Hindus (Macfarlane 1972: 55; Pignede 1966: 217-218). In both instances, they relied almost exclusively on the memories of older villagers for their data on rodi. Similarly, Hitchcock alludes to the waning importance of Magar rodi (1966: 88-90).

Andors takes critical exception to the notion that the demise of rodi is due to Hindu influence. She cites examples of highly Hinduized Gurung villages where rodi is thriving; "there doesn't seem to be a necessary correspondence between Hindu influence and the demise of the *rodighar,"* she writes (1974: 22). She concludes that an explanation of change based purely on Hinduization is simplistic and that such trends may better be explained by looking at the changing socio-economic base of Gurung society.

In fact, both explanations are correct, but must be taken together. Hinduization of the Himalaya is pervasive. It is a larger phenomenon than mere religion and value orientation. With it comes adjustment to new social and cultural patterns. I have already mentioned how the Gurungs have accommodated to economic systems introduced by Hindus, how they have adapted lowland agriculture and changed the focus of their trading. In some villages this is more apparent than in others, and has come, over time, to affect many basic traditions in social interaction as well. In Ghaisu and in the north central Lamjung villages where Andors studied, however, Gurung society has maintained more traditionalism than elsewhere, and rodi associations are still strong, playing vital social, ritual, and economic roles.

In summary, the data on Ghaisu village rodi enable us to appreciate much better the dimensions of rodi and its important roles in society. In addition to its recreational and socializing functions, rodi has served as the basis for certain socio-economic and socio-religious activities with a cooperative, heterosexual, inter-jat basis.

Marriage in Ghaisu

The Gurung rules of marriage can be simply stated: clan exogamy, jat endogamy: one must marry outside his clan, but inside his jat. For Ghaisu and the central Gurungs in general it is safe to say that there are no further rules and that any Gurung may marry any other Gurung, of any clan within his own jat. There are, however, certain preferences.

Pignede, in his lengthy discussion of Gurung social organization (1962) sets more stringent rules within the Char Jat. He, and Macfarlane and Allen after him, describe the Char Jat as a dual system of endogamous pairs - Ghale-Ghodane and Lama-Lamichane - which he feels is a reflection of ancient Hindu influence. (See also the discussion of Western Gurung Char Jat social organization by Doherty 1975: 93ff.) Allen (1973) accepts this concept of duality but points out that the influence is more likely Tibetan than Hindu. Pignede diagrams the rules of marriage among western Gurungs like this (1962: 112):

Figure 3. *Char Jat Marriage Rules, Western Gurung.*

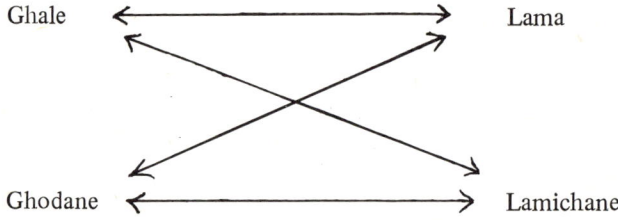

In Ghaisu and Ghanpokhara there is no evidence of this duality in contemporary marriage practice. When questioned, most villagers stated that in their experience Char Jat clansmen could marry with any of the other three clans of the jat. My Lamichane research assistant, for example, has affines among the Ghale, Ghodane, and Lama clans scattered throughout Lamjung District, Bhot Khola in Manang, and in eastern Kaski District. This does not rule out the existence of a duality in the past, nor in contemporary Gurung village elsewhere. Victor Doherty (1974, 1975) supports this view in his lengthy discussions of the organizing principles of Gurung kinship. His Char Jat informants agree that "some

11. The non-Gurung horn-blowers of the Damai or Tailor caste announce the wedding

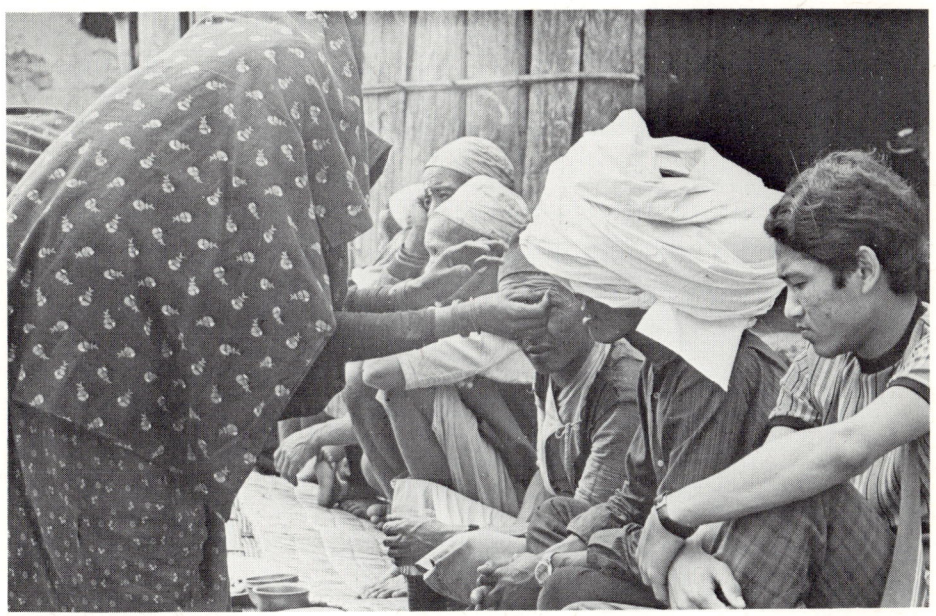

12. The groom, seated with men of his patrilineage, receives a blessing from women of the village

do and some do not" observe the concept of duality in marriage rules. In Ghaisu, only one villager, the assembly chairman who is an exceptionally well travelled and learned man, indicated that the forefathers of the Char Jat followed some sort of rule of duality, but that it is no longer observed. A shematic drawing more accurately reflecting central Gurung Char Jat marriage practices today looks like this:

Figure 4. *Char Jat Marriage Rules, Contemporary Central Gurung.*

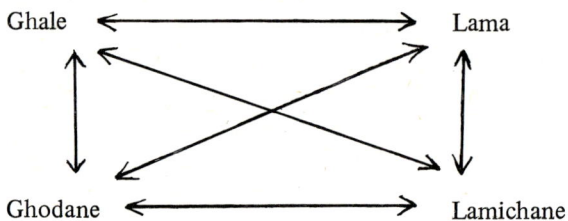

There appear to be no analogous endogamous sub-divisions and hence no analogous prescriptive rule(s) within the Sora Jat.

The basic rule of jat endogamy is given in Legends 1 and 1a (pages 8 ff). To reiterate, the rule forbids inter-jat marriage, then discriminates by absolving ex post facto hypergamy (Char Jat male/Sora Jat female) on the one hand, while fining the Sora Jat male involved in the opposite, or hypogamous, relationship on the other.

There is a marked preference in Gurung society for matrilateral cross-cousin marriage, whereby a boy marries his mother's brother's daughter. To a far lesser degree patrilateral cross-cousin marriage (father's sister's daughter) is also practiced, and although quite rare in Ghaisu and vicinity, it is reportedly very prevalent among some western Gurungs (Doherty 1974, 1975).[10] Pignede found evidence in the Modi Valley that matrilaterality was most prevalent among the Char Jat (1966: 228, 230-233) but he could trace no single instance in succession to a third generation. In Ghaisu, matrilateral marriage is common in both jats. The relationship between the Ghale and the Lamichane clans has already been mentioned. Likewise, there is a long-standing matrilateral cross-cousin exchange relationship between the Yoj of Ghaisu and the Pajyu of Agardi village. Although it was strongly suspected that succession reaches (and quite possibly exceeds) three generations, the data are not conclusive, as the genealogical memories of many villagers are not good in this regard. There is evidence that many trends like these which involve the rules and practice of marriage are locale-specific.

There are essentially two types of conjugal union recognized by the Gurungs:

I call one the 'principal' marriage and the other a 'subsidiary' marriage (after Dumont 1970: 114-116). There are subtle variations as well.

The Principal Union. A principal union among the Gurungs follows the rules of clan exogamy and jat endogamy and is concluded in one of two ways, either by arrangement or by elopment. Arranged marriage is the more common and is particularly important in the instance of a man's eldest son. Elopement, often the result of a relationship which develops in rodi, is far less common.

The arranged marriage has two steps, the bethrothal (*phresyo rhinab,* 'to request the bride') and the wedding (*biya laba,* 'to do marriage'). Each step is accompanied by elaborate ritual and symbolism. Of great importance are the inter-relationships enacted between the lineages involved. The ceremonies will be described briefly to provide the reader with a basic appreciation of the web of relationships, rights, and obligations which are established between two intermarrying parties, and their implications for inter-jat conflict.

The formal bethrothal is arranged indirectly by one or two representatives of the groom's father. The mediator is called *ngebar* and it is he who contacts either the prospective bride's father and his lineage brothers or their own representative(s). After receiving initial approval for the match from the bride's side and having ascertained the horoscopic compatibility of the couple, the groom's representative again approaches the bride's side bringing a gift of *raksi* ('liquor') in a gesture called 'going with the gift of drink' (*jamnar yab*). Should the bride's father and his fellows accept the drink, the match is formally assured and the bethrothal is complete. Because a marriage is so important as an alliance between lineages, the wishes of parents and lineage brothers is paramount. These days, however, young people are being allowed more say in the choice of mates. Then an astrologer is called in to determine an auspicious date, usually during the winter season. Should the father, on the other hand, refuse the gift, then the match is off and the groom's representative must seek a bride elsewhere.

The actual wedding is slightly more elobrate than the bethrothal in that it involves more steps for completion, more participants, and is symbolically much richer. On the evening before the wedding day, the bride is called to her rodi house to partake of the separation meal (*phre kai*). In the morning, or the evening before if the bride lives a long distance from the groom's village, the groom's representatives arrive to fetch her and her party. Again they come with a gift of drink as well as a few rupees to give to the old people who live in her neighborhood. The latter taunt the groom's people for taking the girl away. Meanwhile, the bride's close patrilineal relatives, particularly her father and brothers, and other friends and fictive kinsmen have gathered at her parents' house to perform a separation rite called 'bathing the feet' (*phale khrub*). Some persons give her small gifts of money (*phale khrub mwi*) which are reciprocated later. The bride is then joined by her father, brothers, and other close clansmen and several rodi girl friends, Sora Jat girls in the instance of a Char Jat wedding, and they all set off for the groom's house. They are accompanied on the way by hired drummers and horn blowers of the Damai (tailor) caste who noisily announce the party's progress at prominent points.

Outside the house of the groom, the bride's party is met by the elders of other clans of the village and is sprinkled with rice and water, a gesture meant 'to cleanse the wedding party' (*janti parseb*), symbolic of purity and blessing. Inside around the hearth a number of persons assemble. The bride and groom enter and are seated side by side, flanked by several elder male members of the groom's patrilineage, and by a virgin boy and girl who are in a classificatory son and daughter relationship to the groom and whose parents must be still living. The bride's attendants and a ritualist (shaman or lama) and astrologer are also present.[11] Curious friends and neighbors crowd in to watch. The ritualist gives a long recitation after which the virgin boy and girl feed the nuptial couple fresh yogurt. The groom then touches his bride's hand and give her a white *tika* spot on the forehead, symbolic of purity and union. The others present then apply further tika to both, bestowing their blessings on the union.

The sanctioning of the marriage by the elders of the lineage and by other important villagers is seen in the various acts in which these persons are involved. Their roles were also noted by Pignede (1966: 239), which further strengthens my earlier contentions that units larger than the family, especially the lineage, play critical roles in traditional social interaction and control.

Later, sometimes by several days or weeks, on an auspicious day selected by the astrologer, the final wedding rite of *khi chub* is conducted in which the bride ceremoniously eats her first meal at her husband's hearth, completing the establishment of the new relationship as keeper of his house. Until that time the couple probably has not slept together. Instead, the bride sleeps each night in a neighbor's house accompanied by her girl friend(s), or she returns to her parents' home.

While the rite of *khi chub* establishes a bond of husband and wife at one hearth, the important rite of *te no teb* signals the formal alliance between the two families and lineages in a friendly and reciprocal exchange (*no*). This rite is usually conducted before *khi chub*, although it may be held until the groom's first visit to his bride's parents. The rite has two parts. In the courtyard of the bride's parents' home the representative of the groom performs *phwoli wab,* an expulsion rite during which he jabs a spear into the ground signifying abrogation of

13. A noted dancer from a neighbouring village performs the *jhaure nach*, a Nepali song and dance performed during weddings

14. Wedding feast, consisting of large portions of rice and meat

potential, or real, bad faith or hostility (*phwoli*) between the two parties (analogous to 'burying the hatchet,' the Western idiom for making peace). Next, but not always immediately, the new groom pays his mother-in-law a token brideprice (*chha suka chyob,* literally 'to count six quarters' [Rs.1.50]) of, typically, one rupee only, and a small measure of milk.

During the wedding ceremony, various gifts (*romai* and *kregi kramo*) are presented to the new couple by agnates (of one's own lineage) and affines (of spouse's lineage). Gifts are carefully noted by both sides; their return is expected at a later occasion according to the rules of social reciprocity (*palik*). One who has received *kregi kramo* is considered to have a 'debt outstanding' (*palik cheb*) and failure to return it at an appropriate time in the future may either cause or reflect growing enmity between the two parties concerned.

All weddings are highlighted by feasting. If a man's eldest son is being married a great banquet called *bhater* is prepared and that man extends an open invitation not only to all regular wedding guests but to a representative of each household in the groom's village as well (or at least within his immediate hamlet or ward). For other than an eldest son, a smaller feast called 'hearth invitation' (*chulo nimta*) is prepared, to which only the bride's party is expected to come. In either instance, the new affinal relatives of the groom are the most honoured guests. If the bride is not in the preferred matrilateral cross-cousin relationship to the groom, then the groom's maternal uncle must be invited to attend the feast as a gesture of good will and compensation, for the bride would have been his daughter had a preferential marriage been arranged. Fictive kinsmen must also be invited. If the preferred match was actively sought by one side, only to be refused by the other, then a compensatory gift called *korsi* is also paid as a kind of brideprice (in lieu of marriage) by the boy to the father of the unchosen girl. Compensation, in either instance, varies according to the wealth of the parties involved and how serious the matter is considered to be. It might range anywhere from Rs. 5 to Rs. 30 plus some drink and breads and even a goat or sheep. Compensation is apparently not paid in either Thak or Mohoriya villages (Macfarlane 1972: 42) but it is mentioned by Bista for the Gurungs generally (1967: 73).

In an elopement, the second and less common form of principal marriage, many of the foregoing stages are not applicable. Instead, in place of parental arrangement, the boy makes his intentions known directly by giving the girl a white *tika* mark, after which the couple goes into hiding. In a few days the boy sends his representative (and he himself may go) to the girl's father to reason with him and request him to put aside the affront to his dignity, to cancel what other arrangements he may have sought, and to accept the new relationship. This gesture is called 'to go make up' (*chhyal yab*) and if the bride's father agrees, then his new son-in-law comes with gifts of compensation (*korsi*). The rite of *te no teb*, described above, is performed and the marriage is socially acknowledged. Should the father of the girl refuse, the couple either has to give in to his will and separate, or flees and thereby forfeits all rights and duties vis-a-vis him.

Elopement in Ghaisu is quite rare compared to arranged marriages. It is also rare in Thak (Macfarlane 1972: 129) and a reading of Pignede's long discussion of marriage in the Modi Valley (1966: Chapter 9) leads one to suspect that it is virtually unheard of there. The opposite is apparently the case in Ghachok village near Pokhara where elopement is common, perhaps nowadays even more prevalent than arranged marriages (Jessie Glover, person communication). This may reflect a rejection of tradition, the result, in part, of exposure to the world of modern ideas and new customs in the schools and cinema halls of nearby Pokhara bazaar.

Subsidiary Union. The second type of marriage union, the subsidiary union, has two varieties also, one of *substitution* for the principal marriage that has failed for one reason or another, and one of *cohabitation* of a man and woman of different jats. The latter, of course, violates the rule of jat endogamy. In neither instance is the union formalized by the elaborate ceremony which is so important for the principal union of alliance. With the exception of the cohabitation of a Sora Jat man with a Char Jat (higher status) woman (called hypogamy), subsidiary unions are practically indistinguishable from principal unions and are functionally similar; with the subsidiary union, even that between a Char Jat man and a Sora Jat woman (called hypergamy), affinal relationships are recognized and the attendant obligations and rights are usually honored reciprocally.

A subsidiary union of substitution may occur when a man's first wife is barren and a second wife is brought in to form a polygynous household, or when a couple does not tolerate each other and seeks divorce after which, or because of which, the husband takes a new wife. A second wife may have been 'stolen' from her former husband, in which instance, Nepali law is applied. In one such instance where a Sora Jat man 'stole' the wife of a Char Jat, the offended husband was awarded a settlement of Rs. 1,000 paid by the new husband. The wife stayed with the latter. But this instance, being hypogamous in nature, is not representative of such practices in general. Pignede's description of the situation in Mohoriya is much the same as that in Ghaisu. Most households are monogamous, and there appear to be sincere bonds of love and affection between man and wife. When a man is older and his barren wife agrees, he may bring in a second wife to bear him children. Polygyny, the practice of having more than one wife, is therefore rare, but not untolerated by the society (cf. Pignede 1966: 221).

Only one contemporary case of polygyny was documented in Ghaisu, that of an older and rich former soldier. In that instance, the man's first wife remained with him (she had children) and he built a second room with a separate hearth for the second wife. In Mohoriya, and in Ghaisu, in polygynous households the husband is usually a wealthy man who can afford two wives. In poor families, the barren woman is sent back to her own family and a divorce is announced. The man is then free to marry again. It therefore seems, Pignede concludes (*ibid.*: 221-222), that polygyny only happens when the first wife is barren and if the economic situation allows for it.

The cohabitation variety of subsidiary union involving a man and woman of opposite jats, is not uncommon. It goes uncriticized for the most part, although strictly speaking such a 'marriage' is not permissible by tribal rule. For convenience, cohabitation arrangements are hereafter termed 'common-law marriage,' whether hypergamous or hypogamous. The hypergamous inter-jat common-law marriage is of particular interest in light of certain marital affairs in Ghaisu which are discussed in the context of social conflict later in the book.

Breach of jat endogamy, the rule forbidding marriage outside of jat, is not at all uncommon in Ghaisu, as attested by the number of such regularized unions recorded in genealogical accounts. Nearly five per cent of all marriages recorded (to a depth of three generation) were across the boundaries of jat. Two-thirds of them were hypergamous unions between Char Jat men and Sora Jat women, and the remainder were hypogamous involving Char Jat women. They did not tend to run in family lines, although close male lineage brothers, especially among the Char Jat, were involved in a number of them.

Hypogamy, involving a Char Jat woman, is the more offensive relationship and it is not surprising that few examples of it are found, although one could argue that such relations are simply better kept secrets. Not only is hypogamy sanctioned by stiff fine, as already noted, but the woman who 'marries down' is considered lost to her patrilineage and she becomes a social non-entity to them. Rarely in practice, however, are the personal bonds between brothers and sisters severed with such cold finality.

The incidence of hypergamous unions in Ghaisu and among the Gurungs more widely seems not unrelated to the proclivity among Nepalese and north Indian caste groups (particularly the Rajputs) for hypergamy (see Fürer-Haimendorf 1960; Dumont 1970: 109-125). In interpreting the above figures, however, one should take caution, for if anything they should perhaps be higher. The figures do not include, for example, six documented hypergamous rodi liaisons which are discussed later in the book. Their inclusion here would tend to favour the assumptions made about hypergamy in Gurung society. Furthemore, several villagers when questioned refused to discuss the clan membership of some women in the genealogies. Finally, most common-law unions in Ghaisu appear to have developed out of love affairs in rodi.

Notes

1. Similarly, Doherty (1975: 110) writes that Gurung clan membership "is a very important source of social solidarity."

2. Doherty (1975: 115), studying the Western Gurungs (primarily of Pokhara bazaar and vicinity), indicates that "nowadays Gurungs do not contract *mit* relations except with members of other ethnic groups," but infers that under former traditional village life circumstances *mit* bonds were contracted between the jats. The latter is the case in Ghaisu, giving more strength to my contention that Ghaisu is representative of an older and more prescriptive Gurung situation.

3. The term *rodi* is derived from *ro,* Gurung for 'sleeping' (*roba,* 'to lie down to sleep') and *di,* a corruption of the Gurung *ti,* 'house.' Andors (1974) also suggests that the term *ro* might mean 'friends.'

4. Hitchcock notes the existence of rodi in Magar society and describes them as loosely organized, spontaneous "song and dance groups" (1966: 89-90). The Rang-Bang of Almora, India, which "resembles a Nepalese *rodighar",* is a "social gathering of young boys and girls, generally at night in a house or field for dance, drink and music" (Srivastava 1953: 195n., 193).

    Among all the studies of dormitory associations in South Asian tribal societies, two stand out. One is by Fürer-Haimendorf (1938, 1969) on the Morung of northeastern India, and the other is by Elwin (1947, 1968) describing the Ghotul institution among the Muria Gonds, an Austro-Asiatic tribe living in Bastar, Madhya Pradesh. Elwin calls the Muria dormitory "the most highly developed and carefully organized in the world" (1968: viii).

5. The question of Gurung rodi origins and of earlier, richer forms of rodi-like youth associations has yet to be rigorously researched. Certainly Macfarlane is correct when he states that "it seems clear that the *rodi* were only one feature of a complex age-grade system of which little remains" (1972: 56). His and other studies (Pignede 1966, Bista 1967) leave the impression that Gurung rodi is a mere vestige of an earlier, richer cultural tradition. By comparing my data and that of Andors (1974) with Macfarlane's and Pignede's it appears that the form of rodi extent in at least our two

villages of Lamjung is of a different and probably far older model than that of Thak or Mohoriya villages which they studied.

6. Andors (1974) distinguishes three age groupings, and describes a kind of social metamorphosis or life-cycle "from its first inception, through maturity, until its gradual, but final dissolution."

7. The dividing age corresponds closely with the estimated age of procreative maturity for Gurung girls, i.e. 12 or 13 (and for boys, age 15 or 16) (Macfarlane 1972: 117).

8. Rodi-like youth associations elsewhere in the Himalaya have been said to function "as a means of recreation and entertainment" and "as an agency for pre-marital understanding between boys and girls leading to marriage" (Srivastava 1953: 203). The purposes for Magar rodi (Hitchcock 1966) and for Gurung rodi elsewhere (Macfarlane 1972, Pignede 1966, Andors 1974) are generally the same.

9. Elsewhere nogars are said to function in the performance of such work as cutting and carrying firewood (Macfarlane 1972, Andors 1974) and in house construction (Pignede 1966). Ghaisu villagers, however, insisted that neither of these are nogar functions in the strict sense of the word. Wood cutting and carrying groups are organized annually each winter in Ghaisu on traditional neighborhood and kin group bases, and house building party members are conscripted from each clan in the village according to a code of reciprocity and on the basis of specific individual skills.

10. Doherty (n.d.) argues that patrilateral cross-cousin marriage is the *principle* rule among Gurungs. He bases his conclusions on an extensive study of Gurung kinship terms. Later, in his dissertation (1975), however, he modifies this stand somewhat and concludes that whatever the practice, *reciprocity* is the most important organizing principle of Gurung marriage. Perhaps a case for bilaterality, with localized preferences and a strong penchant for reciprocity (in the form of sister exchange), would rest on firmer grounds.

11. Pignede reports that no priest is present in the ceremony at Mohoriya except for a Brahman in marriages of a Hindu nature (1966: 236). Brahmans never preside at Gurung weddings in Ghaisu.

CHAPTER FOUR
Social and Religious Celebrations

Introduction

A number of ostentatious public social and religious celebrations, organized on village, jat, and clan bases, are held each year in Ghaisu and in similar other villages. These occasions involve large numbers of persons in a variety of roles and specialities. All manner of religious expression - shamanic, Hindu, and Buddhist - are represented and considerable social interaction occurs at these events. By tradition, each celebration described herein involves, to some degree, the participation of members of both jats. Since the ritual specialists play a large role in them, and in a variety of other ritual as well as contractual relationships with laymen, the shamans, astrologers, and Buddhist lamas of Ghaisu are thoroughly discussed. Finally, the dramatic and very public rites accompanying death and post-funerary observations are noted, with particular emphasis on the social interaction considered necessary for their success in appeasing evil spirits and in preparing the deceased for life hereafter, and descendants for the life remaining. Later, it will be shown that it is particularly in these settings that interaction between the jats has been affected by the local status conflict.

The Celebration of Dasai

The great pan-Hindu festival of Dasai (*dasharha* in Hindi) is observed for four days, beginning on the seventh and lasting through the tenth day of the light lunar fortnight in the month of Kartik (mid-October to mid-November). This is a season of family reunions, feasting, and worship. Village pathways are swept clean, houses are freshly mud-plastered, and everyone wears bright new clothing. Dasai usually corresponds with the end of the rice harvest. Given the strong, almost nationalistic character of Dasai in Nepal, all castes and almost all ethnic groups participate. In Ghaisu, it is regularly observed by the Sora Jat, the Char Jat, the Blacksmiths, and the Magars alike.

The two most important events of Dasai are *durga puja,* the worship of the Hindu goddess Durga (or Kali) on the third day, and the bestowal of blessings by the King (or his representatives) upon the populace on the fourth and last day. There are attendant activities on the two previous days preparatory to these main events. Each day's activities are discussed separately as each is traditionally observed, from the perspective of the villagers of Ghaisu.

15. The rite of *tho seba*, beheading the sacrificial goat at Dasai

Initial preparations for Dasai begin earlier in the month with family trips to the bazaar to buy material for new clothing and for sugar, candies, and cigarettes. Soldiers begin to arrive home on leave from the army and migrant laborers return briefly from jobs elsewhere in Nepal and north India. Beer mash and liquor are prepared and stored to be served to guests and friends over the holidays. Clan elders begin collecting expenses from each household for the purchase of water buffaloes or sheep for slaughter. Cattle and sheep herders begin moving their herds down from the highlands so as to arrive near the village in time for the festivities. Throughout the village an air of great expectancy and festive good will prevails.

The first day of Dasai is called *phul pati,* referring to the traditional decorations of 'flowers and leaves.' On this day water buffalo and sheep are slaughtered and the meat is divided equally among subscribing households. During the day, rodi girls gather wild flowers with which to decorate the shrine of Durga.

The second day is *astami,* the 'eighth' of the month. Each family that can afford it privately sacrifices a goat or sheep and hangs the meat above the hearth to dry. Later, on the fourth and final day, a portion of that meat will be offered up when the ancestors are invoked. Meanwhile, some of it is cooked for snacks and to garnish the two daily rice meals. This is a time of great feasting and of food exchanges between fictive kinsmen, real kinsmen, and close neighbours.

The third day is called *naumi,* the 'ninth,' and has two parts. It begins with a morning sacrifice and the worship of Durga, and concludes with a full afternoon of competitive games held on the fields near the school house. The central religious focus is the image of Durga which has been formally enshrined during a midnight ceremony in the village assembly house called the 'house of Durga' (*durga ghar*).

The sacrifice of the day *naumi* is called *tho seba* (or *kat mar*), the 'sacrificial animal cutting.' Armaments and tools are worshipped, from which event the alternative name of 'armory worship' (*kot puja*) is derived. This worship is widely observed by the Gurungs.

During the afternoon athletic competitions are held. They are an annual event and attract young men from villages as far as a day's walk away. Competition is keen in the stone disc throwing contest, the main event. Judging is based entirely on individual physical ability and the youth who throws the stone farthest wins a small monetary prize and the honor of becoming widely known as the winner of that year. Participants are identified individually and by village. The event is not known for any jat or clan altruism.

The tradition surrounding the acquisition of Ghaisu's own image of Durga is the subject of a legend which gives primary ritual responsibility to the Char Jat clan of Lamichane. The legend has two parts, the first of which relates to the origins of the image of Durga. The second part, Legend 5, tells how the local Char Jat clans came to employ Buddhist lamas and is not germane to the discussion of Dasai.

LEGEND 4

Origins of the Image of Durga in Ghaisu

Many generations ago it was arranged for a Lamichane man of Ghaisu to marry a Ghale woman of the village of Taje in Bhot Khola (Manang District). Those were in the days before Ghaisu had an image of the goddess Durga, and the Ghale woman, being a pious person, would not consent to live here unless an image of Durga was brought from Taje. It was done, and henceforth the lineage of her husband has been responsible for keeping the sacred image and for conducting the rituals of Durga Puja during Dasai each year.

The elders of the Lamichane lineage G keep the image in a house in Besi hamlet during all of the year except the last two days of Dasai. On those days it is publically displayed and worshipped at the assembly ground in the main village. The priest (*pujari*) of Durga is a Lamichane man of that same lineage. He dresses for the occasion in a white *dhoti*, a garment worn by Brahman priests. It is he who oversees the sacrifice and conducts the 'armory worship' in honor of Durga. The Lamichane priest of Durga Puja is also a practicing village Buddhist lama. Because of his vows in the latter role, his head is shaven and because, as a Hindu priest, he must have a topknot (*tupi*), he fashions one out of leaves for the occasion. He also refrains from performing the blood sacrifice personally. Another, non-Buddhist, member of his lineage is delegated to behead the goat.

Whereas the third day is primarily one of ritual-religious significance, the fourth day, *tika* (alternately called *dhashami* or *dasai,* 'the tenth') is by and large secular. The only religious activity is the simple ancestor worship, non-Hindu in character, which is called *phaili thhe*. It is conducted privately in the homes of lineage elders. This rite involves invoking the spirits of the deceased, reading the names from the clan ledger (*dapthar*) and offering them gifts of meat. Traditionally, Sora Jat shamans preside at this rite for all local clans including the Char Jat.

Far greater attention is given this day to the visit by each household head to the Jimuwal to receive the King's blessing (*raja ko tika*). Thereafter, the villagers entertain friends and relatives, pay respects to elders and in-laws, and receive their blessings in return.

16. The shrine of the goddess Durga - two gurungs of the *lamichane* clan in attendance as the *pujari* priests

The three Jimuwals of Ghaisu give the King's blessing as part of their official duty; taking it is the right of every householder. While visiting the house of the Jimuwal of one's ward, the villager is given a *tika* of rice and curds on his forehead, while he bows to receive the laying on of hands and to hear the blessing which goes like this: "This is the *tika* of the King, not my own, which I give to you . . . May you be blessed with long life, prosperity, good fortune . . ." This is a duty which comes with the office of Jimuwal; that office, and not his personality or other identity feature, is the focal point of the occasion.

During the afternoon and evening of the day called *tika,* the village men perform epic dances, the Sorathi and the Chalitra. They are customarily performed by men of both jats. Sorathi has been described vaguely as "a particular kind of dance and song peculiar to Gurungs" by both Turner (1965: 623b) and Sharma (1962: 1103b). In 1972 it was danced by several men of both jats. They drew little attention from the villagers and appeared to be dancing for the sheer joy of it. They disbanded after one hour.

The Chalitra dance is the more widely known of the two and is probably based on Sanskrit epic. It is performed by a chorus of men and boys who beat drums, clang cymbals, sing, and dance the stylized hand and foot movements peculiar to it.[1] Practice for the Chalitra is conducted during the afternoon when the dancers and elders gather in one of the larger courtyards of the village. Chickens are sacrificed to Saraswati, the Hindu goddess of learning and the wife of Brahma. This meat is then cooked and served along with quantities of liquor to all the assembled clansmen. In Ghaisu, dance practice is customarily led by a guru of the Lamichane clan.

Towards dusk, the dancing party reassembles according to tradition in the courtyard of the hereditary village headman, the former *khhro,* the elder clansman of the Lamichane lineage A. Two young lads are costumed in feminine garb and take the center positions in front of two rows of adult male dancers, about ten performers in all. The men play drums and cymbals and sing while the boys dance, prompted by the dance guru. Meanwhile, a mat and blanket have been spread directly before the performers for the village elders, leaders, and guests. Large quantities of maize beer are served and spectators present the dancers with small gifts of money and cigarettes from time to time. In this manner, dancing and drinking carry on long into the night.

Ghanto: Gurung Dance-Drama

A second socio-religious event of great importance to Ghaisu villagers is Ghanto dance-drama, an ancient production held each spring during the full moon

17. Girl dancers of Ghanto in their costume (including toy bows and arrows to depict the hunting scene)

day of Jeth, (mid-May to mid-June). Villagers told me that Ghanto may have been performed on the full moon day of Baisakh (mid-April to mid-May) in former times. In 1972, however, it was held from May 28 through 31.

The central feature of Ghanto is a legend reminiscent of the Ramayana epic. The entire production takes four days to complete and is divided into forty unequal parts of scenes. The first eight parts of the story tell about a legendary king and his queen, various events in their lives including the death of the king and the immolation (*sati*) of his queen, and her subsequent return to life. The rest of the production depicts a long and eventually successful hunting venture followed by a gambling spree. It ends with the presentation of a share of the kill to the village headman.

There are at least two variations of Ghanto. The one performed in Ghaisu is called *saidi* Ghanto; another, *baramasya* Ghanto, is performed in Ghanpokhara. The latter we did not see but Ghanpokhara villagers explained that while *saidi* Ghanto is slow and unaccompanied by drumming, *baramasya* has a faster tempo and is accompanied by drums. Similarities or differences between the respective epics is undetermined. The language of the Ghanto chant does not appear to be either modern Gurung or Nepali. Whatever it is, it is quite unintelligible even to the Ghanto gurus who can only say what each part is about generally. The Ghanto guru of Ghaisu thought the language to be Tharu, from southern Nepal.

In Ghaisu, several Sora Jat men under the lead of a guru maintain and perpetuate the Ghanto tradition, supervising the drama, performed by two prepubescent Sora Jat girls, and chanting the accompaniment. The two girls are the objects of elaborate ritual by which they are initially possessed and finally depossessed of the Ghanto deities who appear to depart voluntarily. The girls perform a well rehearsed and highly stylized dramatic dance, maintaining strict silence and wearing elaborate costumes, which vary according to the part of the story. The dancers are prompted by two older attendants who may once have been dancing girls themselves. The performance is staged within a wicker mat hut temporarily constructed for this occasion on the village assembly grounds.[2]

To prepare for and stage the Ghanto, a working committee of boys (*paraphre*) and girls (*ghaneri*) is recruited from rodi youth of both jats in the village. Together these youths are led by three or four older Sora Jat boys, about age 20, who are called *thokne* and who command strict allegiance and respect. Group membership is carried over from year to year with additional recruits drawn annually from among the younger boys and girls. Their responsibilities are to prepare the Ghanto hut and collect contributions of drink and rice from every household for the feasts which accompany the festival. They also supervise and participate in secular

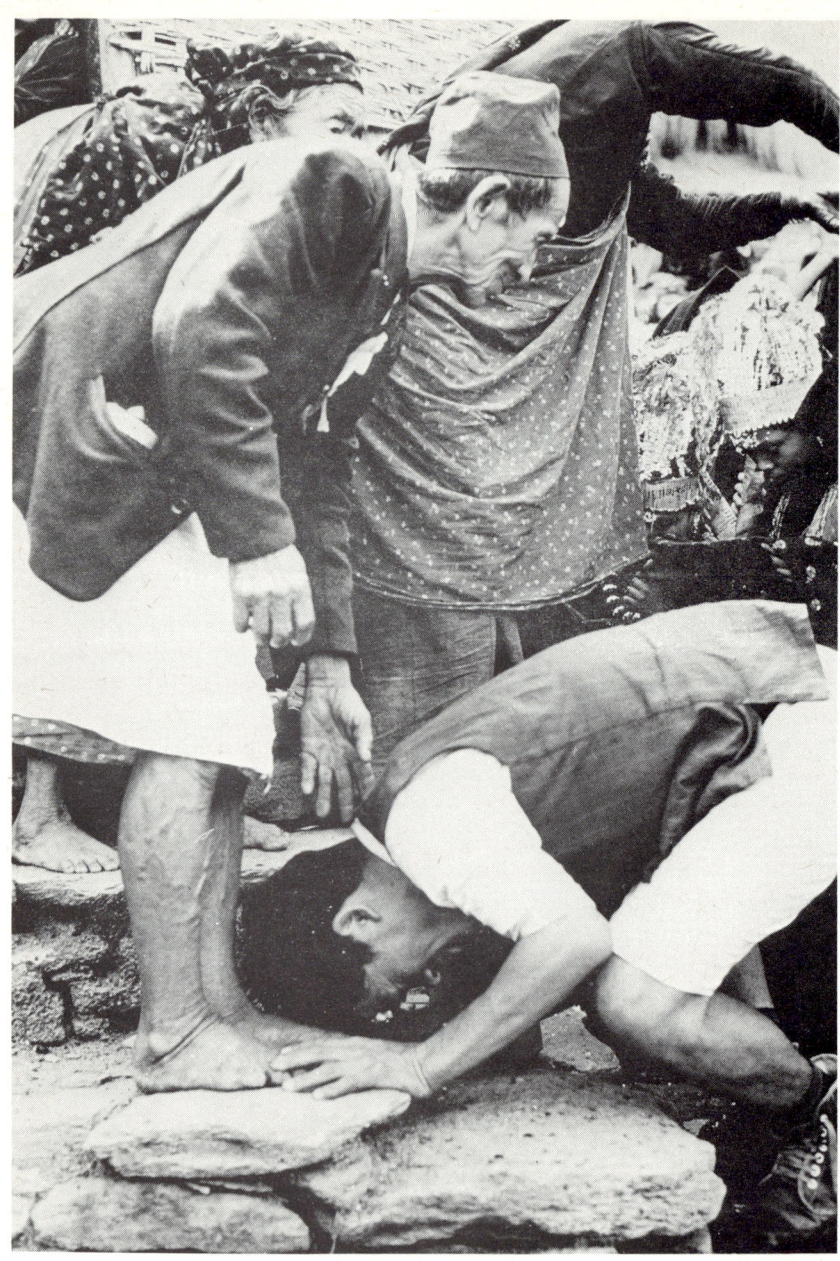

18. The ritual gesture of obesiance called *syo laba*, performed by a young man to the chief of the *Sora Jat*

19. The clowns of Ghanto entertain the crowd, providing comic relief

20. The author with a clown

song and dance (*jhaure nach*) and comic acts (*jogi laba*) which go on simultaneously with, and sometimes even interrupting, the dance-drama. At the end of the Ghanto production, the committee members join in a final ritual which is directed by the Ghanto guru at the edge of the village. There the deities of Ghanto are symbolically released from the performers and reinterred in two simple stone shrines. Finally, after Ghanto is completely finished, the young people take down the stage and hut and clean the assembly grounds.

Throughout the four days of Ghanto, elder Sora Jat clansmen assemble inside the assembly house opposite the Ghanto stage to smoke the *hukkha* water pipe and drink liquor and beer. A spirit of camaraderie exists among these men and no women are allowed to join them. Elders of Ghaisu's Char Jat clans are normally invited to join the Sora Jat men during part of the time. If visitors come from neighboring villages to watch the events, the men among them are also invited into the assembly house for a drink or perhaps to eat some boiled eggs and bread. Guests are given *ashik,* a blessing, and are expected to reciprocate with gifts (*dan*) of cigarettes and a few rupees.

Meanwhile, contributions of money, rice, and flour are collected from most of the households of the village. They are counted and dispersed by the Sora Jat elders. With the money, one or two large water buffalo are purchased and butchered on the last day. A large outdoor kitchen is set up near the upper water spout and during the afternoon when the meat, rice, and gruel, a sort of blood pudding, is ready, each subscribing house sends someone to claim a share, which is then served as the evening meal at home. In this way, all who can afford it share in the feast of Ghanto.

In summary, the performance of the Ghanto ritual and the intimate social interactions of smoking and drinking together by the elders are the exclusive domains of the Sora Jat clansmen, to which others are present by invitation only. These parts of Ghanto are, in a way, the reciprocal of Durga Puja and the day of blessing during Dasai which are primarily Char Jat oriented. But, as during Dasai, other activities carried out in conjunction with Ghanto, such as the preparations by the working committee and the final feast, are shared by members of both jats.

The Non-Hindu Ritual Specialists of Ghaisu

The socio-religious festivities described so far, Dasai and Ghanto, are ostentatious village-wide events, participated in by various categories of persons. Most other ritual-religious occasions, such as life crisis events, are more personal. They are each conducted by particular ritualists and are restricted to a single family, lineage, or clan, although persons of other clans and across jat lines frequently attend. The most important social and religious occasion of this sort is the celebration of death. To fully appreciate the importance of ritual in the society, and particularly the occasion of death, the various non-Hindu ritual specialists of Ghaisu will be discussed first (see also Messerschmidt 1975). They figure importantly in the inter-jat conflict which will be examined shortly.

Sora Jat Shamans. The shamans of Ghaisu come primarily from the Pajyu clan. Their chief guru is a man of the *khepre* class of shamans. He is sometimes joined by a younger brother as well as by an elder of the Yoj clan and a half dozen young disciples (*shiso*).

Two classes of shamans are familiar to my Ghaisu informants (although several other types are known more widely among the Gurungs). They are the *khepre* and the *pajyu*. Note the occupational linkage with named clans; originally, it seems, each class of shaman priest was the speciality of the men of the Khepre and Pajyu clans, respectively.[3] In Ghaisu this is no longer true, for the local *khepre* shamans are Pajyu and Yoj clansmen. The Khepre clan is not represented.

There are *pajyu* shamans of the Pajyu clan living as close as Kinara and Agardi villages, within an hour's walk, and farther distant in Ghalegaun near Ghanpokhara. The *pajyu* shamans seem prevalent among western Gurungs, while more *khepre* are found among the central Gurungs. Apparently *pajyu* ritual is in some ways complementary to *khepre* ritual, although there is evidence to indicate that the *pajyu* may be classified more as exorcists than the *khepre* (Messerschmidt 1975). Pajyu shamans are rarely called upon to perform in Ghaisu; one of the few known occasions is their annual performance of Ghale clan ancestral cult worship called *phaili thhe* for which they are summoned all the way from Ghalegaun.

The principle *khepre* shaman of Ghaisu traces his patrilineal tradition back ten named generations to a forefather who studied at a Bon monastery at Lupra in the Tibetan border region of Lo, in Mustang District.[4] None of the lineage has ever returned to Lupra for further study, although this is the usual practice among other shamans elsewhere. The Ghaisu shaman explains that because his forefather gained such extraordinary insight at Lupra that he passed on to succeeding generations, there is no further need of return for more study.

The shamans possess no books. They pass their lore of esoterica, myth, and ritual down by oral tradition. There is a saying in Gurung which differentiates shamans from lamas in this respect: *tamu pe laba, khepre-mai; chhwe kheba lam-mai* (khepre shamans do Gurung myth; lamas read books).[5]

Unlike the shamans described by Pignede (1966), the Ghaisu *khepre* have no

21, 22. Gurung *kheprẽ* shamans performing the post-funerary ceremony of *pai*

special headdress or other garments. Their paraphernalia consists almost exclusively of a tambourine-type drum and cymbals, rosary beads, and a wooden bird. In addition, a small pottery jug called *pyogu* is peculiar to the Ghaisu *khepre* guru, a potent but very personal symbol (*chinu*) of his ritual identity and authority. This jug has been handed down to each guru in succeeding generations. It was secured by the first shaman in Lupra, according to a legend telling of its magical powers.

The wooden bird, common to all *khepre* shamans, is called *nami*. It is held in the hand or tucked into the waistband when dancing, and it is the one object in particular which every shaman guru carries with him on ritual occasions. The shaman is only eligible to use the *nami* after he has been invested as a guru by his master. Ornithological symbolism is an especially important element of Asian shamanism (Eliade 1964).

The primary roles of the Ghaisu *khepre* guru are to divine and cure illness, to exorcise and control evil demons during the funerary ceremonies, and to prepare the souls of the deceased for their final travels to the land of the ancestors hereafter. They also officiate at all clan ancestor cult worship except that of the Ghales clan, as noted earlier, and on occasion they officiate at smaller, more private rites.

In Ghaisu where there is no Brahman priest (*pujari*) available to officiate at local worship of the Hindu gods Mahadev and Devi and of lesser godlings and forest spirits, the local *khepre* guru fills in. On the occasion of Hindu worship, he dressed in an unsewn white lower garment called *dhoti*, to emulate the Brahmans. He does not go so far, however, as to don the sacred *janai*, the 'holy cord' of the 'twice-born' castes.

The Hindu deities, minor gods, and spirits are considered to be the protectors of the village. When pleased and properly attended, they are thought to bring good fortune to all. Ghaisu villagers worship them jointly on the basis of village membership with few jat or clan distinctions. This worship, therefore, is relatively unaffected by inter-jat rivalry and no attempts have been made on the part of clansmen of either jat to call in Brahmans for prestige purposes.

The Ghaisu shamans also participate in one other ritual context, the worship of certain capricious ancestral spirits for a lineage or clan. This is the category of worship called *bayu thhe*, 'spirit worship,' which involves placating a spirit divined to have caused some type of misfortune, pestilence, or sickness which has affected clan or lineage members. In Ghaisu, there are five clans which have *bayu thhe* of their own (Sora Jat Yoj, Nasi, and Thorche, and Char Jat Lamichane and

Ghale), and a separate, larger *bayu thhe* which receives the attentions of nine of the eleven local clans. The latter is dedicated to two girls, one each of the Ngor and Phle clans, and is called *ngorsyo-phlesyo bayu*. The girls died several generations ago under unnatural circumstances, and are considered to be powerful spirits which have returned to haunt and trouble the living. They are placated twice annually, in ritual which the *khepre* shaman guru oversees. This ritual unites most of the villagers in a common endeavor.

Astrologers. Some Gurungs have a special category of ritual specialists called *paidi*, or 'astrologer,' who determines auspicious dates and times for a wide range of daily, seasonal, and life events. On occasion he is also called upon to interpret and cure illness, based on his knowledge of the horoscope. He is skilled in the use of the Gurung-Tibetan twelve year astrologic cycle (*barga* or *barkha*) described in detail by Pignede (1966, Chapter 15; see also Macfarlane 1972: 229-240 for a full discussion of Gurung ritual techniques to deal with disease and illness). In Thak and Mohoriya villages, apparently, astrologic duties are handled exclusively by the lama or shaman and in some special instances by a Brahman priest (Macfarlane *ibid;* Pignede 1966: 224). In Ghaisu the lamas and shamans know how to read and interpret horoscopes, but they rely on a resident astrologer to make important final decisions based on the Nepalese horoscopic calender. The astrologer's role is an essential complement to their own.[6]

Ghaisu's Sora Jat elder of the Nasi lineage B has long been one of the main astrologers in the village. Since his death in 1972, a younger man of Yoj lineage B has performed most astrologic divinations. The Nasi astrologer was regularly hired by both Sora Jat and Char Jat villagers. Sometimes an outside astrologer, usually a particularly renowned Sora Jat man of a nearby village, is called in. Although there are no Char Jat astrologers in the vicinity, neither is there any reason why a Char Jat man could not become one if he so desired.

Buddhist Lamas. Two young village lamas live in Ghaisu and are the first villagers known to have studied and to practice Tibetan Buddhism professionally. One is a Lamichane man of lineage G. The other is a Sora Jat man of Yoj lineage A, although lamaism is primarily associated with the Char Jat. The Yoj lama is a brother's son to the ultimate Sora Jat elder, the chief of the Yoj clan. The young man's choice of ritual avocation has caused the elder some concern; that, and his anomalous identities as both a Sora Jat clansman and a lama are discussed later.

Both village lamas have studied independently with a Tibetan lama guru of the Nyingmapa sect in a monastery at Nar, in Manang District near Tibet. More recently they have studied with two old and learned lama gurus of the Gurung Lama clan who live in a nearby village and who are also students of the Lama of

23. Gurung lamas reciting the initial rites for the *pai* ceremony of a *Char Jat* clansman

Nar. Although the young village lamas were interested in and occasionally involved in lama rituals over a period of fiteen years each, their formal study at the monastery totals no more than about one year apiece, a few months at a time over a period of three or four seasons.

At most the village lamas are only proficient enough with the Tibetan script to copy and read books. The few books that they own were hand copied during their formal studies. Other paraphernalia include wood blocks for printing mantras (magic spells and incantation) which are considered efficacious at times of illness or misfortune of villagers. White flags with prayer printed on them can be seen fluttering over the housetops of Char Jat clansmen who have recently received ministrations from the lamas. The lamas also use the special robes and headdresses of their sect, as well as a double-sided drum, cymbals, bell, hand drum, and ritual dagger called a *phurba*.

The elder lama gurus mentioned above are distinguished from the young village lamas by their age and wisdom and by the nature of the contractural relations which link them to the Char Jat clans of Ghaisu. They are involved in Ghaisu ritual affairs only at the time of Char Jat funerary memorial ceremonies, at which time the young village lamas act as their disciples. In the absence of these elder lamas, the local Sora Jat shamans have traditionally been called upon to officiate at the funerary events of both jats, while the young village lamas have been relegated to conduct minor household rituals and to recite curative mantras for the sick.

Between the two village lamas there is rivalry over which is senior. Locally, the Lamichane who is the elder of the two monks has been called 'guru' (but never in the presence of his own gurus). The younger Yoj lama, however, has progressed farther in his studies and considers himself, and even by some Lamichane clansmen, to be more knowledgeable of Buddhist ritual than his counterpart. Their relative status has caused some concern among the Char Jat villagers.

Both village lamas have secondary roles, one ritual and the other secular, which they perform in the contexts of particular village celebrations. The Lamichane lama performs as a *pujari*, 'priest,' to the Hindu goddess Durga during Dasai. The villagers see no conflict between his Hindu and Buddhist ritual identities, although the traditional performance of Hindu blood sacrifice is inimical to his vows as a Buddhist monk to respect and preserve life. In the discussion of Dasai recall that he delegated this abhorrent duty to a non-Buddhist brother.

The Yoj lama's secular role is that of resident 'joker' or 'comic' (*jokar, jogi*). His antics are a regular second feature during pauses in the annual Ghanto dance-drama and preliminary to the worship of Durga during Dasai. He performs in gaudy costume and his acts are designed to please the crowd with a mimicry and seeming ridicule of the serious rituals.

Contractural Relations between Ritualists and Clients. Contracts between ritual specialists and lay clients in Gurung society are informal, verbal agreements kept alive by oral tradition from one generation to the next. They exist between the Sora Jat clans and their shamans, and between the Char Jat clans with both shamans and lamas. One of the most important contracts in Ghaisu society involves both the local village shamans and the outside lama gurus, and indirectly the village lamas, employed by the Lamichane and by extension the Ghale. This contract is similar to *jajamani* relations between client and priest found elsewhere in Nepal and which is well described in the literature on Indian society. Among the Gurungs, the *jajaman* or 'patron, benefactor, employer of a priest' is called <u>neb</u> (plural *neb-mai*) and sometimes by the Nepali term *data*. The priest, on the other hand, is called *phhaib* ('Tibetan'?). The contract between them is loosely called by the Nepali term *gaj patra,* literally 'a piece of paper, or document, of a yard's measure,' on which contracts are sometimes recorded.

The origins of the contractual arrangement between the Char Jat, the lamas, and the *khepre* shamans is recorded in this Ghaisu legend:

LEGEND 5

Origins of the Char Jat Ritual Contract in Ghaisu

Many generations ago a local Lamichane ancestor (lineage G) arranged to marry a Ghale woman from the village of Taje in Bhot Khola (see Legend 4). The Ghale woman, when she heard that the people of Ghaisu did not hire a lama at funerals, refused to come here to live.
"I will go to live in the house of that Ghaisu Lamichane only when I am assured that the lama of Nar will be called to conduct my burial and commemorative rites (*pai*)," she said.
The Lamichane agreed and the hiring of the lama at burials and *pai* became a regular Char Jat custom.
The distance between Nar and Ghaisu is very great and because it was difficult for the lama to come for every funeral event thereafter, he entrusted the work to a certain disciple lama, a Gurung who lived in a nearer village. Thereafter, that Gurung lama would come in the Nar lama's stead, except during the monsoon season when rivers were too high and travel even for him was impossible. The Gurung lama in turn delegated the burial rituals to the *khepre* shaman guru of Ghaisu and thereafter the Gurung lama would come only in the fall season to perform *pai.*
As he approaches the village, the lama blows his horn and the *khepre* shaman guru goes out to meet him, spreading a deerskin on the trail for

the lama to sit upon and offering him liquor to drink and one rupee *dan* (gift). Thereafter they enter the village together to perform the ceremonies.

When the *pai* is over, the *khepre* guru sends the lama back on his way with gifts of chili peppers and *timur* (a popular spice).

For breach of contract, the offending party agrees to pay the other one *dharni* (about five pounds) of clarified butter.

The Celebration of Death

No social or ritual occasion or rite of passage is more significant to the Gurungs than funerals and post-funerary celebrations. Funeral ceremonies are lengthy and elaborate affairs involving all categories of kinsmen. Not only are they important as rites separating the living from the dead, but as rites of reaffirmation and re-configuration of statuses and roles among living individuals and of bonds between corporate groups.

It is difficult to improve upon Pignede's characterization of the funerary ceremonies as holding "la place de premier" in Gurung social and ritual life (1966: 340):

> (Le funérailles) cérémonies est, sans aucun doute, la plus importante aux yeux des Gurungs du point de vue social et du point de vue religieux. En fait, pendant les funérailles, le social et le religieux se mêlent d'une menière si complexe et si logique qu'il serait à mon sens inutile, voire faux, de vouloir les délimiter systématiquement pour analyser la perspective gurung. Dans la cérémonie des funérailles, toutes les croyances et institutions gurungs se trouvent réunies, se complètent, s'expliquent. Les prêtres lama, pucu, klihbri officient côte à côte, trait qui ne se retrouve dans aucune autre cérémonie. Les funérailles réunissent non seulement la famille . . . mais aussi des personnes du clan du défunt habitant d'autres villages . . . , des personnes des clans alliés enfin des personnes de clan quelconque, plus ou moins liées d'amitié avec le défunt ou sa famille. Les funérailles affirment à la fois les relations de parenté entre les personnes qui ont un lien avec le mort, les relations entre clans, entre villages, ces relations prenant toute leur signification dans un contexte religieux qui englobe des croyances tres diverses.

> The funeral ceremony is doubtless the most important in the eyes of the Gurungs from both the social and religious points of view. In fact, during the funeral the social and religious blend in such a complex and logical way that it would seem useless, to my way of thinking, to try to categorize them in order to analyze the Gurung way of life. In the funeral ceremony all Gurung beliefs and institutions are found together. The lama, pucu *(pajyu)* and klihbri *(khepre)* priests officiate side by side, which is not found in any other ceremony. Funerals reunite not only the family . . . but also the clan members of the deceased living in other villages . . . , people from allied clans, and finally those people from the clan which is more or less tied by friendship to the dead person or the family. Funerals affirm both family relationships between people who are

connected with the dead man, the relationships between clans, villages, and those relationships taking all their significance from a religious context which embodies many varying beliefs.

Pignede already deals with the funerary events in elaborate detail, viewing them from the standpoints of kinship categories and terminology (1966: Chapter 12) and of the shamans' and lamas' rituals (Chapter 15). His account is generally applicable to Gurung funerary events in Ghaisu, although there are some differences. My objectives here are to present a brief account of the basic funerary events highlighting several specific ritual and social interactions which have special significance for understanding the status conflict in Ghaisu, as well as to contrast the shamans' ritual roles with those of the lamas. Emphasis is on social interactions and practical considerations of the laymen concomitant and subsequent to the religious-rituals, thus complementing Pignede's approach which emphasizes the ritual context and metaphysical considerations.

Gurung funerals are observed in two parts, an initial mortuary rite and disposal of the body (*mhi sibari*) and a concluding memorial ceremony (*pai*). These parts are separated by a transition period lasting from a few days to several months or years, during which mourners are characterized as 'carrying sorrow' (*mri nob*).

The disposal of the body occurs as soon after death as the relatives can be assembled and the shamans or lamas can begin their requisite rituals. Burial or cremation usually takes place within 24 to 36 hours. The transition period is marked initially by signs of great sorrow, but after a few days the mourning and mild pollution which attends death are only observed in token fashion. They are renewed again during the memorial ceremonies and they conclude with rites of purification at the close of Pai.

The Pai memorial is an elaborate series of religious rituals lasting two to three days, followed by a day of conspicuous social interaction (*amel*). The latter day is highlighted by the flow of prestations and the public recognition and reaffirmation of new and old relationships among the survivors and heirs. Amel is climaxed by a great feast given by the agnatic (one's own) kinsmen of the deceased for his affines (spouse's kinsmen).

The closest agnatic kinsmen of the deceased, that is his brothers and/or his sons, are the hosts (*neb*) at all his funerary rites. They employ the shamans and/or lamas and invite and feed all guests and participants. All households in the patrilineage (*tha*) of the deceased and in the wider clan unite in sharing expenses. In Ghaisu it is sometimes customary for several clans to join together to help defray expenses of Pai and Amel, even when they are not themselves ritually involved. For example, in 1972 at a combined Pai of Nasi and Thorche clansmen who died the preceding year, over sixty households of the Yoj, Phle, Ngor, Nasi, and Thorche clans contributed rice, beer mash, and money. This form of lending in the context of a rite of passage is called *paicho*. The one who receives the loan owes a 'debt outstanding' (*palik cheb*), to be reciprocated at a similar occasion. In this way a dynamic reciprocity is maintained, encouraging cooperation between clans. This sort of cooperative financial support is not necessarily jat-specific. Partners are called *pate bhai-mai*, discussed in the context of inter-jat cooperation during Dasai.

Initial Mortuary Rites. When a man dies, an elaborate series of rituals is begun. Immediately at death, his sons and brothers assemble at the house. One of their first acts is to raise a white flat vertically above the house roof. (the flag (*ala*) guides the spirit and alerts others in the village to a death in that household. The cloth from which it is made is given by the patrilineage mates of the deceased.

Throughout the discussion the "deceased" is spoken of in the masculine gender. It is understood that, in general, funerary events for a female are similar to those for a man. Furthermore, because a woman is counted with her husband's agnatic group after marriage, the particular relationships which determine the performance of roles at her funeral are reckoned through her husband, or through her sons if she is widowed. For an unmarried girl, the funerary roles are reckoned through her father.

As the mortuary rituals begin, signs of mourning may be seen among the assembled relatives. Men of the family and lineage of the deceased remove their caps and cut their hair. The women break their bangles and unpleat their hair. Other prescriptions are observed during the period of transition between death and Pai, and during the Pai celebrations.

There are two categories of affines called *asyo* or 'wife-giving' affines who are the real or classificatory brothers to the wife of the deceased and hence of his generation, and *mo* or 'wife-receiving' affines who are husbands to the daughters of the deceased in one descending generation. Pignede defines *asyo* as brother to the wife, and *mo* as son-in-law of the deceased (1966: 275). Under ideal successive matrilateral cross-cousin marriage (sometimes called sister exchange) *mo* and *asyo* are of the same patrilineage but of different generations, and are of *nge*, the matrilineage (as opposed to *tha*, the patrilineage; cf. Doherty n.d.). See Figure 5. In non-matrilateral marriage, the affinal relationships may appear as in Figure 6.

Each category of affine has an important role to play at the funerary events. Several *mo* handle the corpse throughout; they bind it in the shroud (*asyo kwe*) brought by the *asyo* affines, carry it to the cemetery, and prepare the pyre or grave.

FIGURE 5

Affinal Relationships in Preferred Matrilateral Cross-Cousin Marriage

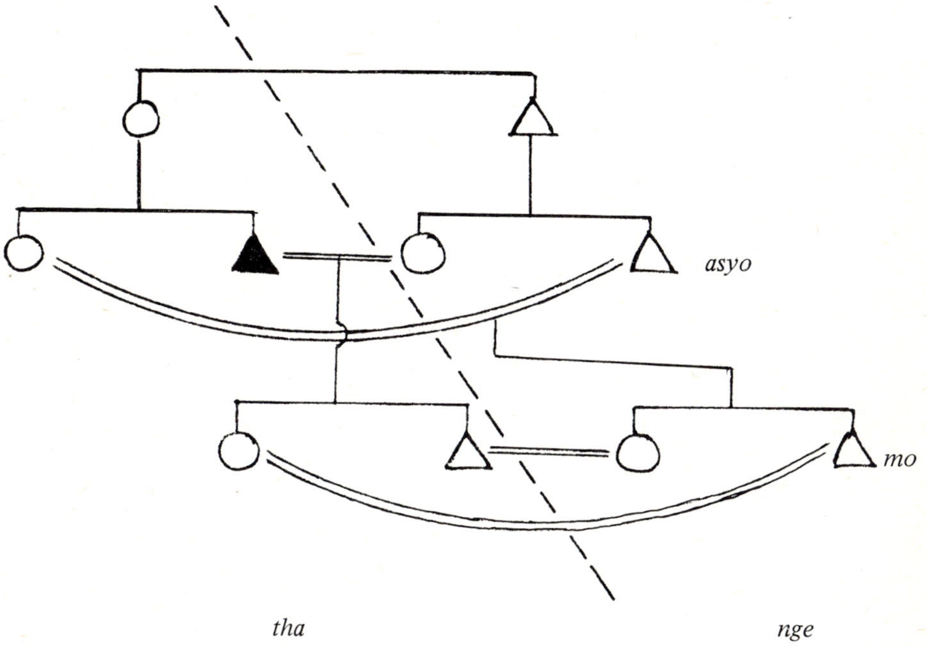

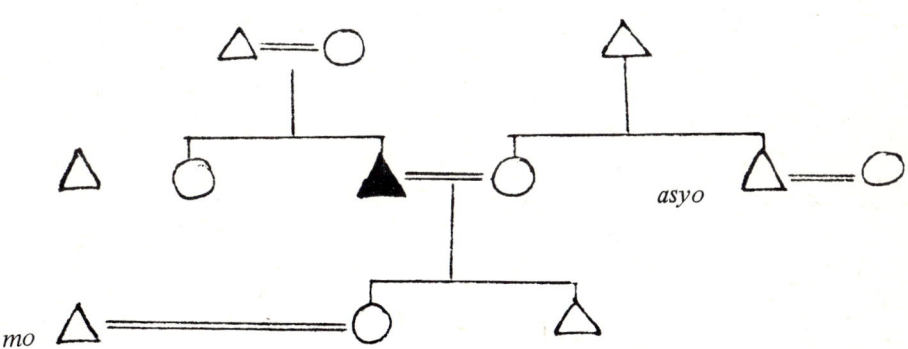

FIGURE 6

Affinal Relationships in a non-Matrilateral Marriage

24. At death a white flag is raised over the house of the deceased

25. Shamans performing their ritual outside the house of the deceased

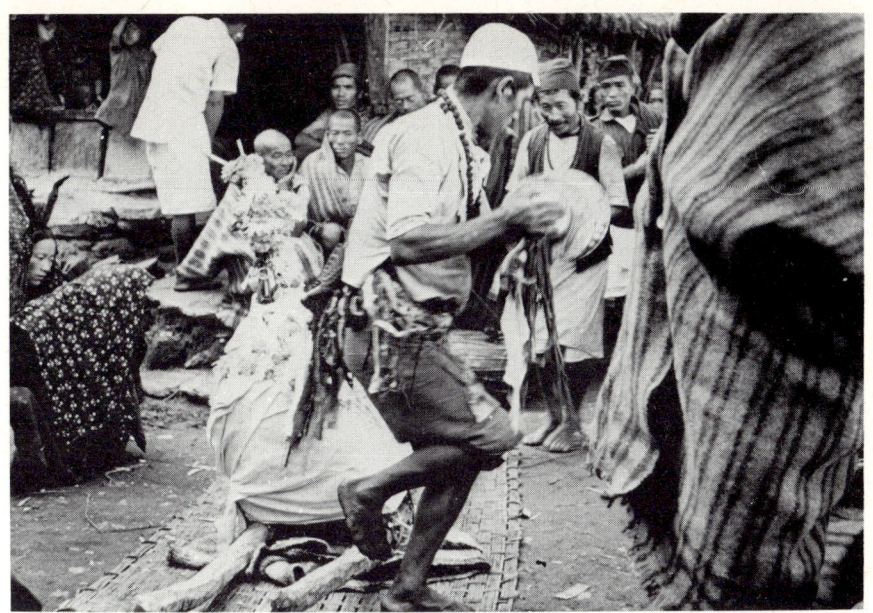

26. The shaman guru performing the ritual of *o nob,* raising his heels over the corpse, an exorcism rite which in this instance caused considerable controversy as the high status Char Jat felt it was demeaning their dead for a low status shaman (Sora Jat) to raise his foot over the body

27. The funeral procession; corpse and bier being carried by the deceased's son-in-laws (*mo* affines)

28. Shamans purchacing a place in the cemetry for the deceased (left, on bier). The shaman guru (lower right with white cap) holds his sacred *nami* - a symbolic wooden bird

29. Real and classificatory sons-in-law of the deceased prepare the funeral pyre

30. Men in the patrilineage of the deceased have their heads shaved at the funeral

31. Visiting lamas with their rich paraphenalia performing a *pai* memorial ceremony

32. Young village lamas reciting from a book at the funeral

33. Young boy mimics his elders at a *pai* memorial ceremony

Burials and cremations are equally common in Ghaisu, although the latter are more expensive and generally reserved for prestigious men. Most women and children are simply buried. There is no difference by jat. The pyres and graves of each clan in Ghaisu are clustered, but there appear to be no distinctions of status according to location.

At a funeral conducted by shamans, they perform their initial rituals inside the house, but soon emerge into the courtyard where a crowd has gathered. The corpse is brought out on a bier carried by *mo* affines and the shaman guru performs a counterclockwise dance about it, raising his feet over the body in a ritual gesture called *o nob* while expelling evil spirits. Thereafter, the shaman guru's feet are bathed by the female mourners and he is given token payment for his services by the patrons of the funeral. Later he is also paid a share of rice.

On the way to the cemetery, a goat is sacrificed to the demons. The flesh of the goat is used in a subsequent ritual of purchasing land from the lord of the cemetery. Later, the meat is cooked and eaten by agnatic kinsmen.

To this point four things differentiate shaman mortuary ritual from that of the lamas. First, the ritual paraphernalia differs. Second, the lamas' books replace the shamans' oral traditions as the repository of requisite knowledge. Third, the lamas perform no dances or gestures resembling *o nob,* where the shaman raises his feet over the corpse. And fourth, the lamas prohibit all forms of blood sacrifice. The importance of these four differences becomes obvious in the discussion of status conflict.

The rest of the mortuary ritual is essentially the same whether conducted by a shaman or a lama. At the cemetery, the body is burned or buried. If buried, the corpse is stripped and the clothing is burned. Likewise, the bier is broken up and scattered. For a cremation, the *mo* affines prepare a pyre and cut large quantities of wood. The body is unbound and laid atop the pyre. The first ember is put to the lips of the deceased by his eldest son, or in his absence another son, real or classificatory. This act is called *dag batti laba,* 'to do the fire brand' and is probably of Hindu origins. Should there be no real or classificatory son available, the son of the deceased's *ngyel* fictive bond brother (or anyone else) can perform the rite. In that instance, the substitute son, like a true son, shaves his hair (including eyebrows and moustache), and receives a parcel of land in compensation, like a measure of inheritance. This land gift is called *dag batti mor misa mro,* the 'fire brand moustache eyebrow field.'

The Period of Transition. The period of transition between the disposal of the body and the memorial rites of Pai is one of mourning and 'sorrow' (*mri*) and of the observance of mild death pollution (*jutho*). The symbolic acts and gestures observed by those 'possessed by death pollution' (*juth laidib*) and 'carrying sorrow' (*mri nob*) tend to overlap. Death pollution touches a wide range or persons, agnatic and affinal, but particularly the wife-receiving *mo* who handle the corpse. To a much lesser degree the pollution affects fictive kinsmen, but whether or not they actually observe any of the proscriptions of pollution and mourning depends upon how strong the bond of brotherhood is considered to be.

Death pollution and mourning are signalled by actions which change the outward appearances of the mourners. At death, the agnatic male (*tha*) remove their caps usually for three to five days, or for as long as 13 days among persons more influenced by Hinduism. They shave their heads and facial hairs at the cemetery. The close female relatives (*ri chame*, 'sisters and daughters' [and wives]) break their bangles and unpleat their hair. Both sexes refrain from eating milk or meat, from engaging in sex, holding a wedding, wearing flowers, or taking *tika*. Affines display no overt signs of their sorrow or pollution except for brief moments during the memorial rites when they respectfully remove their caps. They also bathe and thus purify themselves after the disposal of the body, and the *mo* wash all tools used at the cemetery.[7]

Between the time of death and the final purification rites which conclude Pai (months of years), the agnatic kin observe attenuated mourning proscriptions which amount to little more than abstaining from wearing flowers or taking *tika*, and if the period extends beyond a year even these prohibitions are relaxed.

Some time between a month and a week prior to the beginning of Pai, a rite called *phi krodzeb* is conducted to announce formally the names of the departed and the dates of the memorial rites being celebrated in their honor. This occasion brings together all of the agnatic men, the ritual specialists, and an astrologer. The dates and times of specific events during the commemorative rites are determined by the astrologer from the horoscope and time of death of one of the departed kinsmen, usually the most prestigious man or woman among them. This particular deceased person thus plays a role called *kra nob*, 'head carrying,' referring to his or her honored position as the head or principal departed kinsman being memorialized during the coming Pai. Most often the lay organizer and overall director of Pai, the chief host, is also a close male kinsman of the principal departed person.

Responsibilities are delegated to the agnates (the husband's agnates if the deceased is a woman) who collect the expenses, cut firewood, prepare the feasts, build the hut where Pai rituals are conducted, and beckon the friends and relatives of the deceased. The man who goes off to announce the occasion is called a tongue-twisting *phreje-rhejer prabai mhi,* 'the guest-calling walking man.' Thenceforth, the agnates must again cease to wear flowers, engage in sex, hold weddings, or take *tika*. The preparations for Pai become their total concern. Failure to meet one's obligations in these matters might displease the spirits of the deceased, risk their safe journey to the land of the ancestors, and cause them to bring their wrath back upon the living.

The period of transition between death and Pai is a time of readjustment, a time when the heirs and survivors realign social interrelationships. Finally, after Pai and during the social events of Amel, social identities and statuses which have emerged are publicly acknowledged along with any new configurations of sociopolitical or ritual-religious relationships which may have occurred as a result of the death of a particular person.

The Commemorative Rites of Pai (Arghun). Pai is conceived of by Gurungs to be an occasion of great gift giving, generally from the survivors to their deceased kinsmen, augmented on the final day (Amel) by respectfully honoring those affinal relatives who are in an alliance relationship with the family and lineage of the deceased.[8]

The memorial rites of Pai begin on the day and time announced by the astrologer. They are normally scheduled during the months of Kartik or Mangsir (mid-October through mid-December). Depending on horoscopic considerations, the Pai may be either two or three days long. Most Pai in Ghaisu combined several deceased clansmen and on occasion the deceased of several clans of the same jat. The rituals for such 'combined Pai' *(tu pai)* are normally performed in a specially built wicker hut in a field adjacent to the village. Pai for a single individual is conducted at his home. The following discussion refers to the celebration of a combined Pai.

There are three stages to the Pai rituals: (1) initially the spirits are beckoned and demons of the underworld are expelled; (2) the deceased are feted grandly by the living and are prepared by the shamans or lamas for departure to the afterworld; and (3), finally, they are sent off forever from the environment of the living. The ritualists subsequently expel any lingering evil and the survivors are relieved of their pollution and mourning obligations.

Pignede has analyzed the social obligations of the Pai itself almost exclusively within the framework of ritual, to the neglect of the very important social obligations which highlight its conclusions during Amel, the last day. This has led him to form a restricted interpretation of the flow and counterflow of prestations between one's lineage and one's *asyo* affines (see Figure 5).

During the first stage of Pai, the shamans' priorities are to worship and honor their own patron deity or lord (*khle*), then to invoke the ancestors (*khema*) of the lineage of the hosts. The latter is done with the beckoning of the deceased back from the underworld where the demons have kept them since death. In expelling and appeasing those demons, the shamans and lamas demonstrate their extraordinary control over death and evil. The rites are elaborate and esoteric affairs, and with shamans, they involve a number of blood sacrifices.

For the second stage of Pai, the focal point is an effigy called a *pla* which is constructed by the *mo* affines. Certain types of wood and leaves are used, symbolic of bones, hair, heart, blood and various other body parts. The *pla* is bound in a shroud to resemble the corpse (see Figure 7). It takes on the aspect of the body of the deceased when tiny bits of the nose, tongue, and nails of the body (or ash from the funeral pyre) collected at the time of death are placed within it by the ritualist. These savings are collectively called *rhi*, 'bone' (?). Similarly, the *pla* is given 'the breath of life' (*so*) through the medium of a baby chick placed briefly inside it.

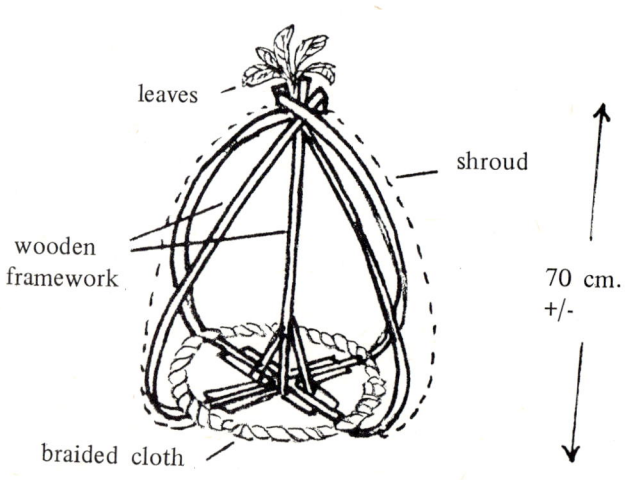

FIGURE 7

The Plan of the pla effigy
(adapted from Pignede 1966: 348)

The emotions evoked by the *pla*, imbued as it is with the spirit of the deceased, are considerable. Pignede describes them well (1966: 348-349):

> Je ne pense pas déformer la pensée gurung en disant que le *plah* fait apparaître le mort vivant aux yeux de l'assistance. Il affirme la vie du mort. Le mort est là au milieu de tous. La veuve s'écroule an pied du *plah*, accablée par la peine. Elle saisit le *plah* et, d'une voix coupée de sanglots, s'écrie: "Pourquoi nous as-tu quittés? . . . Reste avec nous . . Ne pars pas!" Toute l'assistance sent cette présence du mort. Le *pae* prend la forme d'un dialogue dramatisé entre le mort et les prêtres et plus généralement l'assistance.

> I do not believe it distorts Gurung thought to say that the *plah (pla)* makes the dead person alive in the eyes of the onlookers. It affirms the life of the dead person. The deceased is there in the middle of everybody. The widow huddles at the foot of the *plah*, overcome by grief. She seizes the *plah* and, in a voice filled with sobs, cries out: "Why have you left us? . . . Stay with us . . . Don't leave!" All those watching feel this presence of the deceased. The *pae (pai)* takes the form of a dramatic dialogue between the dead person and the priests and, more generally, the onlookers.

All parties to the Pai bring prestations in the form of food, clothing (as shroud), and money which are offered to the deceased and placed on his *pla*. He is told to take each item so as not to hunger, be chilled, or be in any other need whatever. These gifts are claimed by the *mo* affines at the conclusion of Pai, in partial payment for their services. The essential gifts are those given by the *asyo* affines, without which, it is said, the Pai is ineffectual. A legend heard in Ghaisu stresses that under no circumstances can a Pai be performed successfully unless and until the requisite gifts from the *asyo* are forthcoming (*cf.* Pignede 1966: 275). Success is considered accomplished when the deceased safely reaches the land of the ancestors; lack of success is sometimes manifest should a spirit return to haunt the village. The gifts include food (*asyo kai*), drink (*asyo pa*), and the shroud (*asyo kwe*). The latter is presented both at the time of death and at the memorial rites. Furthermore, each gift from the asyo is given at the end of a series of prestations which conclude the participation of laymen in each such ritual.

In Pignede's account, the role of the affines is complete now in the context of the funeral. He concludes (1966: 276) that "celui qui a donné une fille donne, celui qui a reçu une fille reçoit, et agit" (the person [*asyo*] who has given a daughter gives, he [*mo*] who has received a daughter receives, and acts). In Ghaisu, however, prestations to and from the *asyo* affines continue on through the following day of Amel (below).

Preparations for the third and final stage of Pai are being made all along. The shamans or lamas give recitations preparing the deceased for the journey to *lanas,* 'the village of god,' the land of the ancestors. At the conclusion of these recitations the agnates and affines of the same generation of the deceased admonish the latter to take care and go safely and swiftly from them. They enact a ritual called *myar dhurab,* 'turn by turn performing,' during which each actor, called a 'demon stabbing man' (*che to-bai mhi*), takes up a khukuri knife and a spear and, standing before the Pai hut, symbolically drives away the evil which may block the route. Turning around both ways, each man says, in turn (in Gurung):

kya ayosyana kya thodu!
nhe ayosyana, nhe thodu!
e a chhedu, thu aghlodu!
khe ku man ku di kyo!
chhyalne apa rimurchhe (lama rinpochhe)!

If you cannot find your way, open it (with these weapons)!
If you cannot find rest, open rest (take it)!
Do not trouble yourself!
Do not swallow a friend (take none of us with you)!
Go and join the nine grandfathers and nine grandmothers (ancestors)!
O incarnate father (/mother)!

The last to perform this rite is, again, an *asyo* affine. In all their roles as last performers and last gift givers they are called *asyo ka chob,* the 'lid closing affines.'

The *pla* effigies are then carried out of the village by the *mo* affines, accompanied by the shamans or lamas and a crowd of mourners. At the edge of the forest, the ritualist expels any demons which might be lurking along the route to heaven and he informs each of the dead for the last time that he is, indeed, dead and must leave forever. The *pla* are then summarily destroyed and their parts cast into the bushes. The *mo* affines claim all gifts which have been given to the *pla*. A short purification ritual is conducted at the Pai hut and in each of the houses of the deceased, and Pai is complete. The taint of death pollution and the burden of sorrow and mourning are now lifted from the agnates and affines.

Throughout a Pai officiated by a shaman, the recitations of their myths (*pe*) call for blood sacrifice (*tho seba*). These are deemed necessary to appease and satiate the demons during and after rites of expulsion, and to provide the deceased with the necessary 'seed' (of goats, sheep, and chickens) for the life in the hereafter. Although the sacrificial rites are conducted by shamans, the actual killing is performed by the *mo*. The meat is saved and served at small feasts during Pai and at the final great separation feast at the conclusion of Amel for which other animals, usually water buffalo, are also ritually slaughtered.

The Prestations of Amel. Note that throughout Pai prestations from all parties are directed to the deceased, that is to the *pla* effigy which is the focal point of all ritual and social interaction. In effect, the *pla* is the meeting point between the two affinal relationships (Pignede 1966: 278). During Amel the direction of prestations changes. Now various new relationships are recognized and gifts are no longer heaped upon the departed, but upon his living heirs. During the early stages of Amel, when prestations take the form of *kregi kramo*, the living heirs are the center of attention. *Kregi Kramo* is the ritualized gift of a white turban cloth (*kregi*) to a man and a shawl (*kramo*) to a woman, along with a few coins or rupees. A son as heir is henceforth considered the legitimate head of the household, and widows or widowers are now free to remarry. The successors to such prestigous roles as shaman guru, Jimuwal, or village headman are now dutifully and lavishly honored. In short, new roles, identities, statuses, and other relationships between living persons are now publicly acknowledged.

Prestations do not stop there, for the agnates reciprocate with *kregi kramo*, food and drink, and the great feast of *mhi du kai,* 'men together rice.' to which all participants in Pai are invited. After Pai conducted by a lama this feast is called *khheu piba*, 'great gift giving.' The *asyo* are given seats of honor next to the ritual specialists. The hosts of Pai and their wider agnatic kinsmen speak of their duty to please the *asyo (asyo-mai phu laba)*. During Pai they have given the affines their best woollen blankets to sit upon (*asyo-mai bichhyauna*). Now the hosts must give token payment in coin in order to retrieve the blankets.

These gestures represent a final expression of the good relationship of alliance which has heretofore existed between the deceased's lineage and his affines's lineage(s). This is indeed the *a-mel,* the 'dis-uniting' or 'separation' in the literal sense of the word, a rite which marks the end of a specific link. Under usual circumstances, however, the same affinal lineage retains a connection through someone else in the lineage of the survivors, most often through *mo* affines of the next succeeding generation (see Figure 6). Continued good relations are thus nurtured in Amel.

Amel is highlighted by an afternoon and evening of dancing and singing the *serga kwe*, a style of funerary music for which the Gurungs are noted. For miles around one can hear the resounding beat of the double sided bass drums, called *dhaudu*, which accompany the music. The *serga kwe* is typically performed by the adult men of the village and their guests, led by an elder guru. Often during recesses, young boys of the village pick up the drums and mimic their elders. At times the women also perform line dances of their own. These occasions are marked by much laughing and good cheer, and last long into the dark of night.

Notes

1. The Chalitra may be related to the *nachari* ('dance') described by Hitchcock among the Magars (1966: 92-94). It consists of excerpts from the Ramayana and from the life of Lord Krishna. Just as with the Chalitra in Ghaisu, the patron goddess of the Magar *nachari* is Saraswati. In the village of Hitchcock's study dancing was allowed only during a special season which began on Krishna's birthday in September and concluded at the spring celebration of Saraswati Puja in February.

2. Pignede describes Ghanto as he heard about it from an old guru who was in charge of the last production in the Modi Valley at Ghandrung village, near Mohoriya in Parbat District, thirteen years before (1945?). His data differ from that of Ghaisu in only minor details. From Pignede's account and those of various Gurung villagers, the tradition seems to have died out among the more westerly Gurungs during the last generation and is now, apparently, performed only in Lamjung District, and perhaps in Gorkha District farther east.

3. For categories of shaman: *khepre* and *pajyu* (italicized, lower case); for clan names they are rendered Khepre and Pajyu (unitalicized, capitalized), respectively. Similarly, lama (anglicized) is the category of Buddhist monk, while Lama (capitalized) is the Char Jat clan of the same name.

4. Lupra is a small Bhotia-Tibetan town in the region of Lo, Mustang District, behind the Annapurna Range and along the upper Kali Gandaki River north of Thak Khola. It is several days' journey northeast of Gurung country. According to Tibetologist David Snellgrove, Lupra (*Klu-brag* in Tibetan) is the site of the oldest Bon monastery in that region (1967: 84n.). It has been identified as White (reformed) Bon (*bon-kar*) as opposed to the older Black Bon (*bon-nag*) by Corneille Jest (personal communication). Bon is the pre-Buddhist shamanic religion of Tibet. The references to Lupra by the *khepre* shamans and others of Ghaisu and Ghanpokhara give strength to the suggestions by both Pignede (1966: 387 ff.) and Macfarlane (1972: 227) that Gurung shamanism is derived from Tibetan Bon.

5. *Tamu* is the Gurung term for themselves (pl. *tamu-mai*).

6. By way of caution, neither the Gurung *paidi, khepre,* nor *pajyu* ritualists should be confused with either the Nepalese *jhankri* or *dhami*. The latter are defined as "diviner, conjurer, wizard" and as "wizard, sorcerer" respectively by Turner (1965: 231b, 327b) and are described as men who become possessed (Pignede 1966: 293; Macfarlane 1972: 225). Some villagers referred to the *pajyu* shaman loosely as being "just like a *jhankri*" but without possession.

7. Pignede's account of the funerary observations among western Gurungs is curious for its almost total neglect of pollution and mourning. He mentions only in passing that the men cut their hair and the women unpleat and wash their's and he interprets all washing more as acts of hygiene than of purification (1966: 69, 276). Either he did not observe the more stylized and symbolic aspects of pollution and mourning, or they are considerably less important in Mohoriya than in Ghaisu.

8. The Nepali term *arghun* is frequently used in place of *pai,* and holds essentially the same meaning of gift giving. One linguist has interpreted it to be related to an Indo-Aryan term, *argha*, meaning 'the respectful reception of a guest,' or 'respectful offering' (Ruth Schmidt Plunkett, personal communication, 1974). Note that the Gurung term *pai* is similar to the north Asian Teleut term *pairam*, the 'funerary banquet,' which in turn may derive from the Persian *biaram*, meaning 'festival' (Eliade 1964: 208n.).

CHAPTER FIVE
Jat Interface – Conflict and Change

Introduction and Overview

Social conflict has been defined as "a struggle over values and claims to scarce status, power and resources in which the aims of the opponents are to neutralize, injure or eliminate their rivals" (Coser 1956). Status is "a combination of rights and duties" (Goodenough 1965), such as those inherited by the Char Jat in terms of social superiority, economic and political leadership, and by the Sora Jat in the realm of shamanic responsibilities and as subordinates to the Char Jat in economics and politics. Status defined in this fashion implies privileges, powers, liabilities, and immunities in the context of social interaction, within and across social boundaries (ibid.). One may also speak of "status identities" and "status relationships." Some important status identities among the Gurungs include those of Mukhya, Jimuwal, shaman, clan elder, and so forth. They operate in such relationships as Mukhya to villagers, Jimuwal to taxpayers, shamans to clients of both jats, and elders to clansmen. There are, of course numerous other relationships between individuals and corporate status groups, sometimes embracing multiple identities. They are the stuff of social controversy, dispute, and conflict.

Claims to scarce high status and the reconsiderations of values and social transactions dominate the conflict that developed in Ghaisu. Briefly, the Sora Jat aimed to redefine their corporate status, to eliminate status distinctions, and to reorient . . and in some instances to eliminate, as we shall see . . certain transaction patterns altogether across the boundaries of jat. They began to draw upon the new egalitarian phrasings of Nepal's new Village Panchayat Act, as well as on other claims to embody ethnic Gurung traditions. The Char Jat strived, on the other hand, to defend their high status distinctions as well as the traditional status-bearing transactions in question, i.e. to maintain the status quo.

In time, however, the Char Jat became aware that their opponents were at least partially successful in permanently changing some of the dominant status-bearing relationships by breaking with tradition. In this chapter, I will describe when, how, and why certain serious breaches of Gurung tradition occurred in Ghaisu. The Sora Jat were assisted by changes at the national administrative level (beyond local control) in the form of government directives which have eliminated the Char Jat's sole claim to certain village political functions and economic privileges. As a consequence, the Char Jat began to try to maintain their alleged higher corporate status identity by other means, calling upon other cultural alternatives. Some of their claims to status precedence are cast in traditional Hindu-Buddhist phrasings drawn from the larger society, and in great measure from Gurkha soldiery.

Neutralization of opponents claims have been the clear resolve of both parties to the conflict.

Conflict concerning relative status of each Gurung jat is not new to Ghaisu, nor to Gurung society at large. It has been noted by others and has been documented to have been a tribal-wide issue as early as 1854, and specifically in the villages of the Modi River Valley in Parbat and Kaski Districts as early as 1908 (Pignede 1962). Pignede was the first anthropologist to write in detail about inter-jat status conflicts. He relates incidents which he personally observed in 1958 and he has recorded others recalled by his informants. In some instances, grievances over status discrimination were taken to court; in others, not; but in every instance the sides were clearly drawn along jat lines and the issues were heatedly debated. In short, acknowledgement of a status conflict is not new.

In the writings of both Pignede and Macfarlane, two factors emerge as explanatory: (1) the alleged superiority of the Char Jat as founded in legendary tradition and supported by historical court action, and (2) the fact of Char Jat economic superiority. Macfarlane (1972: 37-38) writes,

> It was during the nineteenth century that most of the legal battles between the two classes took place, in these they attempted to work out their relative status and how they were to treat each other. This possibility reflects initial contacts. The period coincides with the founding of many new villages, including those in the Modi Valley where Pignede worked. The reconstruction of the history of both Thak and Mohoriya supports Dr Allen's [1968] hypothesis that it was the members of the *carjat* [sic] who first arrived and thus obtained the best land. Though they are said, in Thak, to have brought a few *sorajat* servants from a particular clan, the majority of the *sorajat* clans came in several generations later . . . . .
>
> [Today, beneath a superficial amity in Thak,] there is a bitterness, especially between old-established *carjat* families which are losing land and those *sorajat* households where a successful army career has brought in a large amount of cash.

One Char Jat elder told Macfarlane that in years past certain Sora Jat clansmen carried his loads and acted as his servants. They do so no longer, and the informant "spoke bitterly" of the change (*ibid.*).

105

Pignede's informants considered it inappropriate for him to ask about inter-jat rivalry or to seek the jat or clan identity of an individual. He concluded for Mohoriya village in 1958 that the servile role of the Sora Jat did not exist except in old and questionable traditions. He relates examples of Sora Jat clansmen portering for the Char Jat and working in their fields without any shade of servitude. Rather, he asserts, such portering and work is determined by economic necessity. In summary, Pignede (1962: 117) writes,

> the Solahjat [sic] are not the servants of the Carjat. They have exactly the same rights as the latter (I am not here speaking of the marriage rules). All the Carjat, or nearly all, recognize this fact in good faith. It is perhaps surprising therefore, that such a controversy should exist between the two groups of clans. I believe that the real motive of the disagreement between the Carjat and the Solahjat is economic. In general, the Carjat are well off or rich; the Solahjat badly off or poor. The Carjat own a great proportion of the land, while the fields of the Solahjat are usually small.

Macfarlane, returning briefly to Pignede's research site in 1969, found the issue considerably abated and he had no trouble collecting census data concerning individual and corporate identities by kinship and descent.

The economic situation in contemporary Ghaisu is much the same as in Mohoriya, and the status rivalry is similar to that in Thak, as far as can be determined. That is to say that the Char Jat of Ghaisu, particularly the Lamichane, dominate the resources, with few Sora Jat clansmen in their wealth bracket, and also that a servile role of Sora Jat toward Char Jat has come to be expected (to a point). The status issue centers on the same historical social and economic disparities, in Ghaisu as well as generally throughout the northern Lamjung region. Contrary to the Char Jat loss of resource dominance observed in Thak, however, in Ghaisu the Char Jat remain relatively dominant despite initial control of the local resources by the Sora Jat in the early history of the village and the equal opportunity to amass wealth through military service more recently. The Sora Jat clansmen, steeped in a strong respect for tradition, have generally but begrudgingly accepted legendary authority in the matter. Unfortunately, from their perspective, those well kept legends, pseudo-historical accounts, and court actions have set historical precedent. Recently, however, antagonism over political rights and roles has arisen following national government administrative reforms aimed at village level government. As a result, certain Sora Jat elders have begun to dispute vociferously the long held claims of Char Jat superiority. The issue has affected nearly all aspects of village life, even some of the most mundane interpersonal ineractions.

In the long run, it has not been the economic disparity alone which is at the root of the Ghaisu conflict, but the general issue of status in all of its domains, economic as well as (or perhaps *particularly*) political and social. The potential of

Sora Jat village leadership, despite economic disparity, inherent in the new Panchayat system is not lost on the Sora Jat clansmen. They understand that by the ideals of universal suffrage wrought by the new Constitution of Nepal they have every right to aspire to and attain council seats by free election and ultimately to gain the village chairmanship itself. Furthermore, their rights extend to social relationships, in that no person is inherently subservient to another because of birth in one or another jat. In short, the Sora Jat are awakening to the fact that the caste-like hierarchical status distinctions are no longer valid in the larger national polity and society, hence should not be at the village level either.

In the following discussion of the conflict development in Ghaisu, I shall begin by describing recent political developments which gave impetus to certain parties in the village to bring the underlying status conflict out into the open. From there, in the following sections, I shall relate the development of the crisis to the point of apparent and irreparable breach of relations between the jats in Ghaisu.

Recent Political Developments

Change in the political power and privilege of village headmen and of local land tax functionaries began throughout Nepal in the 1950's. Far-reaching administrative reforms occurred in two stages.

In 1951, all unpaid labor was abolished and the land revenue collectors lost a major source of manpower to work their lands, the only form of compensation for their services to the government. Not until 1955 were they finally authorized to claim 5 per cent of the local annual land revenues as salary (Regmi 1963: 131).

The second change came with the 1962 Village Panchayat Act (*Gaun Panchayat Ain, 2018*). By this act, village assemblies (*sabha*) were organized (Section 3). Some new administrative units were delineated, incorporating several hamlets and/or villages as one. (Ghaisu and Besi, for example, were combined with Kinara, Agardi, and Talo as one administrative unit with five wards.) Each new village assembly consisted of all the citizens twenty-one years of age or over (Section 5). Eleven representatives were elected from among them to form a Gaun Panchayat or 'village council' from which, in turn, a chairman (*pradhan panch*) and a vice-chairman (*upa-pradhan*) were chosen (Section 18; see also Rose and Fisher 1970).

The preamble to the new law reads as follows, from the Nepal Law Translation Series 1/71 (Nepal, 1962):

A Law Enacted to Make Arrangements Relating to Village Panchayats

Whereas it is expedient to organize Village Panchayats in villages which constitute the lowest stratum under the Panchayat system, have the rural people participate in greater measure in local administration through the Village Panchayats thus formed, make it possible for them to attain economic, social and cultural development in accordance with the age and existing needs, and thus maintain peace and stability by enabling them to adjust themselves to a truly democratic system and modern circumstances, in the belief that the all-round development of national life is possible only through the principle of decentralization of authority, and that such decentralization will have strong foundations and be fully accomplished only through the gradual development of the Panchayat system,

Now therefore, His Majesty King Mahendra Bir Bikram Shah Dev has enacted this law under Article 93 of the Constitution of Nepal.

Two further excerpts from the Panchayat Act will serve to illustrate the discussion below concerning universal adult franchise and the possibility of any man or woman, of any Gurung jat, being elected as chairman or vice-chairman of the Gurung village panchayat:

Section 5. Conditions for Membership of Village Assembly

All persons who have ordinarily resided within the area of the Village Assembly for one year, or who possess residence of their own therein, and have attained the age of twenty-one years, shall be entitled to become members of the Village Assembly.

But no person shall be entitled to become a member of the Village Assembly in the following circumstances:-

(a) If he is not a citizen of Nepal
(b) If he is of unsound mind.

Section 18. Formation and Establishment of Village Panchayats

(1) There shall be an Executive Committee consisting of 11 members including the Chairman, the Vice-Chairman and 9 members in every Village Assembly, and such Executive Committee shall be known as the Village Panchayat.

(2) The Village Assembly shall elect the Chairman and the Vice-Chairman from among its members through secret ballot . . .

At first there was no real change in the nominal powers and functions of rural administration, a condition noted throughout Nepal (Rose and Fisher 1970:

79-83). Locally, the greatest innovations were in the adoption of the new administrative nomenclature, and not in political process or structure. Ghaisu's former village headman, the Mukhya, a man of Lamichane maximal lineage A, was simply appointed by unanimous acclaim as the council chairman. He held that post until he formally retired in 1970. He was replaced by a Lamichane of lineage D, the elder half-brother to the third Jimuwal tax collector (see Figure 1).

By all accounts, the former Mukhya was and still is the most respected man in the locale. He is often described as a mediator and peacemaker. This stance has gotten him into trouble with some of the more outspoken of his own Char Jat clansmen, particularly with the new council chairman who maintains a strong defensive posture in the face of recent Sora Jat redefinitions of status. Despite criticism from traditionalists, however, the former Mukhya and his younger brothers, both of whom are among the six wealthiest villagers in Ghaisu (Table 5), have encouraged close personal ties with certain poorer Sora Jat clansmen. Their relations with the Sora Jat are personal and cannot be considered patron-client; they are not manifest in ritual settings. One effect has been a partial split of the ranks of the dissenting Sora Jat.

The new council chairman is not an especially well liked person, but was elected primarily because of his known knowledge of administrative, political, and economic affairs. He has lived and worked in Kathmandu and is a wealthy man by village standards, a local moneylender, and one of the leading landowners. He, too, is one of the six wealthiest men in Ghaisu, along with his younger half-brother. Both brothers are outspoken opponents of Sora Jat aspirations, a curious posture for the chairman whose mother was a Sora Jat. Curious, that is, until one considers that given the chairman's marginal birth status he has become rigidly orthodox in a drive for acceptance.

At the time of his election as council chairmna, it was thought that he, out of all possible candidates, could best speak for Ghaisu Panchayat in a dispute over jurisdiction over some forest land claimed by a neighboring village panchayat. When the case came up in 1972, Ghaisu lost and the chairman's popularity, already low, suffered more.

Theoretically, any adult villager is eligible for election to the Gaun Panchayat council and he may then aspire to the chairmanship. In fact, the Char Jat have retained and defended their dominance. In the present (1972) alignment of council seats, seven are held by Char Jat and only four by Sora Jat, although the population ratio by jat is the reverse. This demonstrates, in part, the tremendous prestige and power that the Char Jat maintains in the locale despite their minority.[1] The pattern of a dominant few retaining power is commonplace. "So far, the

109

traditional elite groups of rural Nepal have usually succeeded in maintaining control over the local councils, *but their dominance has not gone unchallenged"* (Rose and Fisher 1970: 82; emphasis added).

In the eyes of the Sora Jat the new Panchayat system has given them hope of being able to ascend to the village headmanship. Now they see the possibility of one of their own number achieving the village council chairmanship, in the face of status deficiency. It is this possibility, however remote, which has prompted them in great part to challenge the status quo.

For the present, however, the new system has resulted not in gain, but in a loss of the small power of the Sora Jat through their clan chiefs (*chiba*). In decisions of a purely local village nature, that is, within Ghaisu and Besi, the headman traditionally consulted with the clan chiefs of both jats before taking action. The former headman, when chosen to chair the new council, continued that practice. His replacement did not, but on occasion made decisions without their representative counsel. Although he is not bound by law to act upon the advice of the informal council of chiefs, failure to poll them before making local decisions is viewed as a break with tradition. A major incident involving just such nonconformity occurred in 1970, causing consternation among the Sora Jat leaders. The ensuing dispute triggered a crisis in political relationships rapidly involving the membership of both jats at large.

The incident happened just before the celebration of Dasai in 1970. Three events occur almost simultaneously in the fall of each year: (1) the harvest of soya beans, a petty cash crop, (2) the arrival of the shepherds back from the highlands, and (3) the celebration of Dasai. They usually occur in that order, allowing sheep and cattle to graze the fallow bean fields for a few days while the shepherds reunite with families and participate in the festivities. Thereafter, they descend to winter pasture down the valley. In 1970, however, the beans had not yet ripened in time for Dasai and when the shepherds were about to arrive, the beans were still in the fields. Several concerned villagers, Sora Jat and Char Jat alike, approached the council chairman privately and asked him to make a directive prohibiting the shepherds from turning their herds loose in the beans. That decision was quickly made and the authority to announce it publicly was delegated to a Sora Jat man of the Ngor clan. The shepherds were advised to stay their arrival until after the beans were harvested, hence until after Dasai.

When Yoj and Nasi clan chiefs, whose own shepherds and sheep were affected, heard the announcement they became angered that the decision had been made without consulting them. It was done secretly, it seemed to them, without their personal knowledge. They publicly reproached the council chairman, demanding that he retract the directive. Instead, he stood firm against them and the decision held.

The concern of the Nasi and Yoj elders turned more on the principle involved than on the inconvenience to shepherds. The chairman's decision was interpreted as a slight not only on the two angered elders, but on the good counsel of all the clan chiefs combined. It was also interpreted as an attempt to gain new powers for the chairmanship, at the expense of the Sora Jat. In reaction, the Yoj and Nasi elders, gathering strength from other Sora Jat clansmen beholden to them, elevated personal animosities to the level of village politics. They ultimately made their feelings felt in virtually all inter-jat social and ritual ineractions. This, the bean field dispute, set the stage for the series of crises which follow, disrupting social, political, economic, and ritual interactions throughout the village.

Crisis Development

The entire status-oriented affair in Ghaisu followed the pattern of a "social drama," as described in a study of conflict development by Victor Turner (1957). Turner posits four distinct phases in the progressive enlargement of social disturbances to full scale conflict (1957: 91-92). These four stages are useful in describing the development of conflict and crisis in the Ghaisu case. They are:

> 1. "Breach of regular norm-governed social relations ... signalled by the public breach or non-fulfilment of some crucial norm regulating the intercourse of the parties" involved.
>
> 2. A "phase of crisis" during which the breach has a tendency to widen "until it becomes coextensive with some dominant cleavage in the widest set of relevant social relations to which the conflicting parties belong."
>
> 3. "Adjustive and redressive mechanisms, informal or formal, are speedily brought into operation by leading members of the relevant social group." They vary situationally according to the unique circumstances and in scope according to the seriousness of the conflict.
>
> 4. "Reintegration or ... recognition of irreparable breach."

Each of Turner's four phases of crisis development will be discussed for Ghaisu in turn. Phase one, the "breach of regular norm-governed social relations", dates to the time of Dasai, 1970, following the bean field dispute described above. It was reflected, as well, in the subsequent performance of the Ghanto dance-drama the next spring.

CHANGES IN FESTIVAL INTERACTIONS

Dasai. Smarting under the chairman's bean field decision, the Sora Jat elders called a secret meeting of the clansmen at which the angered chiefs succeeded in persuading their fellows to boycott all forthcoming Dasai ritual, specifically that directed by the Char Jat toward the goddess Durga. Thenceforth, they characterized Durga Puja as an exclusively "Char Jat affair." Their actions were at once a challenge to the authority of the council chairman and to all Char Jat clansmen in general. It reflected Sora Jat disdain for his, and, by extension, their privileged status. It also reflected growing Sora Jat disaffection toward the Char Jat over concurrently revealed breaches of jat endogamy involving Char Jat boys and Sora Jat girls, and led the elders to impose further restrictions on many other inter-jat associations and activities, particularly in ritual contexts.

In 1970, and again in 1971, the events of Dasai revolving around the worship of Durga were boycotted by the Sora Jat. One of the initial changes involved the Sora Jat Rodi girls and the Char Jat elders. It is customary on the day of *phul pati* for Sora Jat girls to collect flowers in the forest with which to decorate the shrine of Durga. In return, the Char Jat clan elders give them as a group a portion of sheep slaughtered for the occasion. Provoked by the Sora Jat reaction to his directive to the shepherds, the council chairman let it be known that henceforth the Char Jat would not provide the meat, using rising costs as his excuse. Sora Jat girls, some of whom had already collected flowers (in ignorance of their chief's order forbidding it), refused to give them to the Lamichane priest; and since that time only Char Jat rodi girls have prepared the floral decorations.

During Dasai it is also the custom of the clans, except Ghale, to kill and feast on a number of water buffalo. The Ghale slay sheep. Because of the expense and the large amounts of meat involved, two or more clans often join together to purchase the beasts, sharing the expenses through joint subscription by household. The partner clans in this cooperative effort are called 'leaf (?) brothers' (*pate bhai-mai*) or alternately as 'brothers two to the sacrifice' (*bhai ngi tho seba).* The traditional patterns of cooperation between the clans in this instance has been:

1. Lamichane and Lama (Char Jat) + Phle and Tu (Sora Jat)
2. Nasi, Ngor, Thorche, Kromche, and Pajyu (all Sora Jat)
3. Yoj (Sora Jat, large enough to afford the costs alone)
4. Ghale (Char Jat, who butcher sheep instead of buffalo)

The Phle and Tu (1) are small clans and not as wealthy as their Char Jat brothers, nor are the Lamichane and Lama large enough clans together to handle the expenses for a buffalo and consume all the meat. By this old tradition of splitting the expenses between clans, each household in the village can afford to subscribe without serious financial strain. But given the size and the cost of a mature buffalo (Rs. 200-400), no single clan, with the exception of the Yoj (No. 3), can afford eat one by itself.

Cooperative 1, which involves both jats, was curtailed by the bean field dispute and its repercussions. By 1972, however, that cooperative was functioning again, its clan members sharing the cost of a large female buffalo and her yearling calf, as part of a general trend toward gradual amelioration of the conflict.

Ghanto. Restrictions on jat interactions were not limited to Dasai ritual and cooperation, but were evident during the Ghanto dance-drama production in the spring of 1971. Ghanto has been described as primarily a Sora Jat occasion, but always with liberal Char Jat participation in social affairs. Char Jat boys and girls have served alongside Sora Jat youth on the working committee, in performing secular songs and dances, and in the comic skits that mimic parts of the Ghanto hunting scene. They also took passive part in the Sora Jat rituals honoring Ghanto deities.

Since the bean field dispute of 1970, however, Char Jat participation in Ghanto has been prohibited by both sides. In the 1971 Ghanto, Char Jat youth were not invited to assist the working committee, nor were Char Jat elders invited to join the Sora Jat elders in smoking the water pipe; neither were Char Jat clansmen requested to contribute to the expenses, nor join in the Ghanto feast. All villagers were free, however, to be spectators.

The following year 1972, a few months before the scheduled Ghanto performance, one of the most outspoken Sora Jat chiefs, the Nasi elder, died. Since that time some of the enmity between the jats has diminished (see below, the Epilogue). Toward the end of the last day of Ghanto that year, for example, several more liberal Sora Jat elders suggested that they invite certain Char Jat clansmen, particularly the important men of each lineage, to sit with them. The suggestion was not favored by all of the Sora Jat men, nor with any particular enthusiasm by the Char Jat. Those Sora Jat elders who promoted the idea finally adjourned outside the assembly hut, leaving the dissenters inside. There appeared to be no hard feelings between them, just an honest difference of opinion. Outside, near the Ghanto stage, mats and blankets were spread and several Char Jat men came to join the Sora Jat. It is not clear whether all of the Char Jat elders were invited, or only a select few, but in the end all of the Lamichane lineages except lineage D, that of the unpopular council chairman, were represented.

No similar accommodation for the Char Jat youth was evident. Rather, the few Char Jat youths who came to watch the production of Ghanto for brief periods openly ridiculed the participating Sora Jat boys. At one point, an invitation arrived from a neighboring and predominantly Sora Jat village asking the Char Jat of Ghaisu to come visit as guests of their Ghanto committee. There was some talk of going, but an elder Lamichane told the Char Jat youths to stay at home and carry on as if nothing special was happening.

One important symbolic feature of Ghanto is the overt display of deference paid to the elder Sora Jat clansmen and particularly to the Yoj chief (Yoj lineage A). This 84-year old man is a former Ghanto guru who has passed his knowledge and responsibility to a younger clansman. During the dance-drama now he sits with the younger guru adjacent to the stage, smoking his water pipe and overseeing the whole affair. Following the last scene, the dance troupe, attendants, and members of the working committee go in procession to the edge of the village to release the Ghanto deities. On the way, they stop at the Yoj chief's house to receive his blessing. Two boys carry the dance girls on their backs, and they and other youths and older persons each perform a symbolic gesture of deference called *syo laba*, by bowing the touching their foreheads to his feet. This gesture implies obeisance, and subservience, and the utmost of respect toward the elder.

In 1972, concern for jat status took precedence over the status of age-wisdom and *syo laba* has become an act of respect which the Char Jat no longer wish to exhibit toward any Sora Jat. The avoidance of *syo laba* provides a strong incentive not to rejoin the working committee, even should the Char Jat youths be reinvited. In the past, little thought was given to *syo laba* in this context, but it was a strong and respected tradition. Now, in the emotionally charged atmosphere of conflict and status reevaluation it has taken on greater significance.

BREACH OF ENDOGAMY

Other breaches of norm, tradition, and tribal law occurred almost simultaneously in Ghaisu to enlarge Turner's first phase of crisis development (*op. cit.*). Among them were flagrant breaches of jat endogamy, requiring boys and girls to marry within their own jat, and concomitant changes in the organization of rodi associations.

During 1969 and 1970 several incidents occurred involving rodi youths of both jats in sexual misconduct, striking at the basic Gurung marriage rules. These rodi incidents created village-wide public dismay and prompt reaction from adults. Initially, the dispute between the jats was a relatively narrow one, among several individual primarily. But in their quest for allies, each party sought a broad base of support and backing. Each side began to draw upon inherent positions of influence within the traditional social networks of the village. The rodi sexual offenses were important in generalizing the quarrel, in polarizing parties along jat lines, and the connotation that servile labor (*gha karni*) has derisive sexual overtones may have broadened the impact of this issue.

Breach of jat endogamy is not new to Gurung society. Indeed, it is probably common to all societies where marriage rules honor caste, clan, or class boundaries for the rules to be broken periodically. In Gurung society, such a breach of tribal rules must be understood in terms of the legends and pseudo-histories which some believe to account for the origins of the status hierarchy.

Had only one or two girls become pregnant the affairs might have been, as in past years, quietly accommodated. Instead, in the short span of less than two years, illegitimate children were reportedly born to six Sora Jat girls, fathered by three Char Jat boys. All of the boys were members of the 'Seven House Lamichane' lineages (see Figure 1) and are bearers of the combined status, privilege, and wealth that their birthright implies in Ghaisu.

The only other recent instance of breach of jat endogamy involves a Sora Jat boy and a Char Jat girl in a hypogamous liaison. The boy and girl each paid a small fine to the council of clan elders, but were not married. The child born to them subsequently died and the incident is of no account or concern any longer.

As soon as the pregnancies were known, the Sora Jat elders demanded that the responsible Char Jat boys marry their daughters. When several of the illegitimate children died at or shortly after birth, one of the alleged fathers was immediately freed from further responsibility, thus diminishing the Sora Jat demands. In the instance of a second Char Jat boy who allegedly fathered another of the children, a Sora Jat youth soon implicated himself as biological father and married the girl. The Char Jat boy subsequently married a local Ghale girl by the proper arrangement.

The third boy's case is more complicated. Although two of his alleged offspring died, two lived. The responsibility for fathering one of them, a boy, was conveniently admitted by a Sora Jat youth who married the girl; their child is considered now to be a Sora Jat clansmen. The other living child, a girl, is being raised by the unwed Sora Jat mother, the daughter of a prominent Nasi clansman. The child is recognized and accepted publicly as a Lamichane child and will be expected to marry a Char Jat boy when she is of age. Meanwhile, the marriage of her mother is being considered with a Sora Jat man in the village. Her status as an unwed mother has had no affect on those arrangements. It is significant that the girl's father, the Nasi clansman, has close personal ties with some members of the boy's lineage. The father has also spoken out strongly against continuation of the disruptive confrontation led by his elders in the Sora Jat. His voice, although not that of a clan chief, is all the more effective given his position 'in the middle,' so to speak, as father of one of the girls involved in an illegitimate liaison.

Regardless of whether or not those involved in such breaches of jat endogamy marry or not, they are expected to pay fines for their offenses to the council of clan chiefs of both jats in the village. In these instances, all of the boys involved paid from Rs. 100 to Rs. 200 each, while the girls paid half those amounts.

Particularly vexing to the Sora Jat clansmen was the ultimate refusal of the Char Jat boys to marry the pregnant girls. Except in the instance of incest (marriage within the same clan), any boy responsible for a girl's pregnancy is expected to marry her and most often does.

One instance of incest was recorded in Ghaisu where the boy and girl were of the same clan. The boy was heavily fined (Rs. 1,000) by the council of chiefs and the girl was stripped of her social status as a Gurung and driven from the village. If such a couple chose to live together they would be forced to take up residence elsewhere, in a place where they might conceivably keep secret their true identities. Flight to the resettlement areas near Chitwan in the Rapti Valley near Narayan Ghat at the south or to Bhot Khola near the Tibetan border in Manang District at the north are likely alternatives. Where any such union is known to exist in a community, the offenders are refused commensality and are treated as outcastes. Their offspring are considered to be like the Gharte caste, formerly slaves.

Macfarlane (1972: 119) has described the situation for the Gurungs in general when he writes that in Thak village,

> If a woman is found to be pregnant before marriage ... she would be shouted at and occasionally hit by her parents, but she would not be turned out of the house. She would be forced to admit who was responsible. If the man was eligible for marriage, then the pair should marry, and if either party refused he or she would have to pay a fine of the same size as in a divorce case. Eighty rupees to be paid by the woman, forty rupees by a man are the basic sums, though they might be higher if one partner was really eager to marry. If the partners were respectively from *sora* and *carjat* [sic], theoretically endogamous, they should still marry. But if they are from the same clan ... then they would have to pay a very heavy fine ...[2]

In Gurung society no less than in Hindu caste society, hypergamous unions (Sora Jat girl/Char Jat boy) bring a measure of prestige to the girl who 'marries up' and indirectly to her patrilineal kinsmen (see Dumont 1970: 116, Fürer-Haimendorf 1960). In the instances of Ghaisu, where the boys are heirs to wealth, power, and prestige, there was all the more incentive for Sora Jat fathers to insist on their regularizing the unions.

This latter consideration probably holds true only in instances where there is a measure of demonstrable wealth in the Char Jat lineage involved, that is, where status hypergamy is reinforced by economic hypergamy. The potential advantage of the hypergamous relationship in the lineage of the girl is realized at death, burial, and funerary commemorative rites of one of their number. At those occasions the affines, particularly the daughter's husband (*mo*), reciprocate for the gifts of daughters and sisters as their wives by offering certain prestations and service (see Figure 8). Social prestige in the eyes of one's fellow jat-mates accrues to the kinsmen of the deceased in their displays of respect and honor toward the affinal guests.

FIGURE 8

Flow of Prestations from mo to Wife's Patrilineage in Hypergamous Union

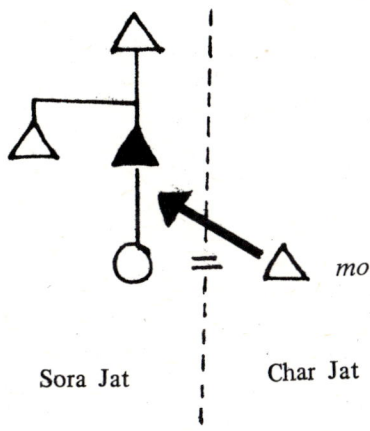

Sora Jat   Char Jat

REORGANIZATION OF RODI

One immediate effect of the conflict over breach of jat endogamy was the restricting of rodi associations in Ghaisu, and changing the membership patterns of nogar cooperatives and tetar theatre troupes. Those rodis which were formerly mixed-jat were reorganized in 1970 to become jat-specific. At the same time, Sora Jat girls were told not to invite non-Sora Jat boys to their rodi houses. Given the disdain which many Char Jat boys now hold for the Sora Jat in general, it is unlikely that their association with any Sora Jat rodi groups will occur now or in the near future within Ghaisu.

On Table 7, the membership alignments in nine rodi associations organized between 1950 and 1972 are shown by clan and jat. Rodis numbering 3 through 8 are shown as composed (A) before and (B) after reorganization.

Rodi 1 was organized in 1950 as a young girls' *kol-mai* rodi, progressed through the *theb-mai* rodi status as the girls grew older, and was disbanded naturally in 1962. Some of its members are the mothers of contemporary (1972) rodi girls. An older girls' *theb-mai* rodi existed in Ghaisu in the early 1950's, but little information about its organization and membership could be recalled by the few ex-members who remained in the village.

In the mid-1950's, Rodi 2 was organized. During the decade of the 1960's six more rodis, numbering 3 through 8, were founded. By 1970 there were seven active rodi groups in the village. Membership in all but two of them reflected the free association of both jats. Only the exclusively Sora Jat rodis number 5 and 7 were exceptions, although there was no restriction on inviting Char Jat boys to their houses. In 1970, rodi 2 disbanded naturally and rodi 3 (organized in 1962) was also nearing dissolution with only two of its members remaining unmarried. In 1970, in the midst of the disruptive social and ritual events, rodi 3 was reorganized and became exclusively Char Jat by incorporating Char Jat girls from rodis number 4A, 6A, and 8A. The single Sora Jat girl in rodi 3A transferred to Sora Jat rodi 5B. In 1972, a new rodi, number 9, was organized for young Char Jat girls, thus perpetuating the new trend of jat exclusiveness.

In one reorganized rodi of each jat (Char Jat rodi 3B and Sora Jat rodi 5B) there was some membership loss. In most instances the girls were married in the interim and their attrition was natural. In at least one instance, however, a pregnant Sora Jat girl dropped out in part because of her intimate role in the jat conflict issue.

Table 7. Rodi Membership in Ghaisu Before and After 1970.

Rodi 1	Rodi 2
Char Jat	*Char Jat*
Ghale 2	Ghale 2
	Lamichane 3
Total Char Jat 2	
	Total Char Jat 5
Sora Jat	
Yoj 5	*Sora Jat*
Nasi 4	Yoj 4
Phle 1	Nasi 1
	Ngor 1
Total Sora Jat 10	
	Total Sora Jat 6
Grand Total 12	Unaccounted for 2
	Grand Total 13
Dormitory household: Sora Jat	
Organized: 1950	Dormitory household: Sora Jat
Disbanded: 1962	Organized: mid-1950's
	Dissolved: 1970

Rodi 3A (before 1970)	Rodi 3B (after 1970)
Char Jat	*Char Jat*
Lamichane 5	Lamichane 6
Ghale 3	Ghale 5
Total Char Jat 8	Total Char Jat 11
Sora Jat	Grand Total 11
Phle 1	(Sora Jat member transferred to Rodi 5B)
Total Sora Jat 1	
Grand Total 9	Note: This reorganized Rodi drew membership from Rodi 3A, as well as transfers from 4A, 6A, and 8A.
Dormitory household: Char Jat	
Organized: 1962	
Reorganized as 3B (across)	

Table 7. Rodi, continued ...

Rodi 4A (before 1970)	Rodi 4B (after 1970)
Char Jat	(Char Jat members transferred to Rodi 3B)
Lamichane 3	
Total Char Jat 3	*Sora Jat*
Sora Jat	Yoj 5
Yoj 5	Phle 3
Phle 3	Nasi 1
Nasi 1	Ngor 1
Ngor 1	Total Sora Jat 10
Total Sora Jat 10	
Grand Total 13	Grand Total 10
Dormitory household: Sora Jat Organized: 1964 Reorganized as 4B (across)	

Rodi 5A (before 1970)	Rodi 5B (after 1970)
Char Jat	*Char Jat*
none	none
Sora Jat	*Sora Jat*
Yoj 4	Yoj 8
Nasi 3	Phle 1
Phle 3	Pajyu 1
Pajyu 2	
	Total Sora Jat 10
Total Sora Jat 12	
Grand Total 12	Grand Total 10
Dormitory household: Sora Jat Organized: 1964 Disbanded: 1970 (See note across)	Note: Although 5A disbanded, a new Rodi was organized in the same household including girls never before in Rodi and one transfer from Rodi 3A.

Table 7. Rodi, continued . . .

Rodi 6A (before 1970)		Rodi 6B (after 1970)	
Char Jat		(Char Jat members transferred to Rodi 3B)	
Ghale	2		
Lamichane	1	*Sora Jat*	
Total Char Jat 3		Yoj	3
		Nasi	3
Sora Jat		Pajyu	2
Yoj	3	Phle	1
Nasi	3		
Pajyu	2	Total Sora Jat 9	
Phle	1		
Total Sora Jat 9		Grand Total 9	
Grand Total 12			
Dormitory households: Sora Jat Organized: 1965 Reorganized as 6B (across)			

Rodi 7A (before 1970)		Rodi 7B (after 1970)	
Char Jat		*Char Jat*	
none		none	
Sora Jat		*Sora Jat*	
Yoj	4	Yoj	4
Nasi	3	Nasi	3
Thorche	2	Thorche	2
Phle	1	Phle	1
Total Sora Jat 10		Total Sora Jat 10	
Grand Total 10		Grand Total 10	
Dormitory households: Sora Jat Organized: 1965		No change from Rodi 7A.	

Table 7. Rodi, continued . . .

Rodi 8A (before 1970)		Rodi 8B (after 1970)	
Char Jat		(Char Jat member transferred to Rodi 3B)	
Ghale	1		
Total Char Jat 1		*Sora Jat*	
Sora Jat		Yoj	4
Yoj	4	Nasi	3
Nasi	3	Pajyu	1
Pajyu	1	Phle	1
Phle	1	Thorche	1
Thorche	1	Total Sora Jat 10	
Total Sora Jat 10		Grand Total 10	
Grand Total 11			

Dormitory household: Sora Jat
Organized: 1968
Reorganized as 8B (across)

Rodi 9

Char Jat

Lamichane	4
Ghale	3

Total Char Jat 7

Sora Jat

                none

Grand Total 7

Dormitory household: Char Jat
Organized: 1972

THE BREAKDOWN OF FICTIVE KINSHIP

Turner's second "phase of crisis" (*op. cit.*) began to show with the breakdown of fictive kinship ties in the village society. It really began with the change from interpersonal confrontation to conflict on a corporate group basis. This phase "exposes the pattern of current factional struggle within the relevant social group . . . . and beneath it there become visible the less plastic, more durable, but nevertheless gradually changing basic social structure . . ." (*ibid.*). In reaction to the initial breach of good and traditional relationships, further changes and redefinitions of a variety of interpersonal and intergroup relationships in both ritual and non-ritual contexts were pursued reciprocally, until a sort of schismogenesis set in - reaction to reaction to reaction (by both parties) - as the whole conflict grew to proportions both unexpected and unwanted by many of the ordinary, especially the poor, villagers. As the quarrel enlarged, it threatened the traditional and highly valued links across the lines of cleavage in the society, the jat boundaries. Rodi was reorganized, fictive kinship broke down, performance of certain categories of labor and services were prohibited, laymen-ritualist interrelationships were interrupted and changed, and funerary ceremonies were modified. It also threatened the very basis of economic stability and social solidarity, so well developed among the Gurungs. Eventually all villagers were involved in one or more ways in the conflict and its ramifications.

At first, as we have seen, the inter-jat status conflict was restricted to the more public social interactions, that is, to festivals and rodi activities. Fictive kinship, it was thought, was a personal relationship between two individuals and in a general way between clans and jats, and would not be greatly affected. In the late fall of 1970, certain Yoj clansmen invited their Char Jat bond brothers to attend the Pai commemorative rites for their deceased clansmen of the past year. Unexpectedly, the Char Jat chose not to attend, and when they avoided the final feast during Amel in particular, the Yoj and other Sora Jat clansmen became alarmed and angered. Not only was this a serious slight on the hospitality and pride of the Yoj, but it signalled the negation of one of the strongest traditions, severing the ties of friendship and cooperation inherent in bond brotherhood.

Following that incident, the Sora Jat elders held a secret meeting at which the chiefs spelled out three rules which would apply unequivocally to all Sora Jat men, women, and children in Ghaisu:

> 1. No Sora Jat would henceforth attend any life crisis events of the Char Jat.
>
> 2. On no account would a Sora Jat carry a Char Jat's personal belongings to a wedding or perform other labor or services for a Char Jat.

3. No Sora Jat shaman would be allowed to officiate at a Char Jat ritual of any description, else he would be liable to a stiff fine of Rs. 200 payable to the council of Sora Jat chiefs.

The following year, 1971, the Lamichane clan held a Pai memorial for the wife of the wealthy and prestigous second eldest brother of maximal lineage A. The widower had a strong fictive kin bond with a wealthy ex-soldier of Yoj lineage E. Despite that, and in light of the Sora Jat ruling, the Lamichane deliberately did not invite a single Sora Jat bond brother to attend. This was a further indication that, indeed, they fully intended to abrogate their fictive kinship relationships.

Quite clearly all villagers of Ghaisu were now implicated in the widening conflict, "coextensive with [the] dominant cleavage in the widest set of . . . social relations" (Turner, *op. cit.*). It was no longer an affair of a few feuding men and rodi youth. Each of the three rules laid down by the Sora Jat chiefs was a dramatic step away from tradition.

CATEGORIES OF LABOR AND SERVICES

The employment of "adjustive and redressive mechanisms," Turner's third stage in crisis development (*op. cit.*), began with the enactment of the three rules mentioned above. They are detailed below according to their manifestations in the performance of labor and services, in changing layman ritualist relationships, and in changing funerary ceremonies.

The rule against performing labor and services for the Char Jat was interpreted broadly to apply to ritual services as well as to economic services. Hence, it threatened not only socio-ritual tradition, but the cooperative work relationships which are integral to the village's well being. Macfarlane (1972: 37-38) speaks of a lingering institution of patron-client relationship in Thak Village which is based essentially in the jat hierarchy. According to this system, when the Char Jat clans first settled in Thak, Sora Jat servants of a particular clan accompanied each of them. There is no indication of such institutionalized relationships in Ghaisu, either now or in the past. The unique circumstances of Char Jat settlement in Ghaisu at the instigation of the Sora Jat were not conducive to it. In nearby Ghanpokhara village, however, a long-standing patron-client relationship still exists between some of the wealthy Char Jat clansmen and Sora Jat 'workers' called *kaji*. The *kaji* system appears to be ritual-specific, but the data are insufficient to define its contemporary lines or its origins. In Ghaisu there is an important distinction between Char Jat/Sora Jat patron-servant relationships and landlord-laborer relationships reflecting economic disparity. The distinction has become all the more clear to villagers by the status conflict and the ongoing contingencies of a subsistence economy. Patron-servant relationships fall within a category of servile labor considered to be demeaning, and sometimes polluting, and are, as a rule, manifest in ritual settings.³ Landlord-laborer relations are in the category of wage and cooperative labor, and are restricted to field work, house building, and the like, for which there are few alternatives should they be discontinued. And, because they are normally between individuals, they do not classify as the same as group cooperative associations.

The origins of the labor and services controversy can be traced directly to the legendary promise of the Sora Jat to perform certain obsequious and deferential services to the Char Jat (Legend 1a). Servile labor is expected in the context of Char Jat rites of passage, weddings in particular. In a Char Jat wedding, Sora Jat men and women are expected to carry the palanquin and the *kalas* of the bride, respectively. In actual practice this has meant that Sora Jat men are paid, or otherwise compensated, for carrying the loads of the Char Jat clansmen attending weddings, and that young Sora Jat girls serve as attendants to Char Jat brides. Serving in the capacity of a mediator in Char Jat weddings arrangements is also included. The category has been further extended by association to include demeaning and polluting service at funerals, specifically when a Sora Jat man substitutes for a Char Jat son-in-law (*mo*), or for the son of a deceased Char Jat man by performing *dag batti* in return for the gift of the 'firebrand moustache eyebrow field.'

Macfarlane notes that at a Char Jat wedding a Sora Jat girl is expected to carry gifts of rice and beer (perhaps analogous to carrying the *kalas*), for which she receives a gift. In other contexts food and utensils are never shared by the jats (1972: 37-39). No instances of refusal were observed in Ghaisu, but it was obvious that most potential food-sharing contexts between the jats were avoided.

Pignede (1962: 115-116) often saw Sora Jat men carrying loads for Char Jat clansmen, but he concluded that the motives were purely economic and not controversial. In Ghaisu it is apparent that economic considerations overshadow all others for the poor villagers, but that in the hostile atmosphere of the status conflict, otherwise neutral interactions began to take on significant meaning and were manipulated by both sides to promote their own ends.

The full implication of the prohibition against labor and services was felt in one instance during the winter of 1970-71, when two prominent Sora Jat men of the Nasi and Ngor clans were invited to attend the wedding of a Lamichane friend in a distant village. These two men were fictive kinsmen of members of the groom's lineage. They attended the wedding without concern for the restrictions imposed in Ghaisu, assuming them irrelevant to an event so far distant.

After the two men had returned to Ghaisu, the Sora Jat chiefs convened a secret meeting at which the men were accused of performing servile labor at the Char Jat wedding. A heated argument ensued and in the end the two clansmen were forced to pay token fines of Rs. 2 each. This incident may be considered a turning point in the dispute between the jats, for villagers have said that the two accused were so angered and affronted by the leaders that they chose to challenge them openly, questioning the merit of pursuing the confrontation with the Char Jat any farther. When members of the 'Seven House' Lamichane lineage heard this, they privately offered the two Sora Jat clansmen economic and moral support should they ever be ostracized from their jat. This incident created a rift within the ranks of the Sora Jat.

It should also be noted that the Nasi clansman involved is the same Nasi whose daughter was involved in liaison with a Char Jat boy, and who already voiced some concern at the continuation of conflict, mentioned earlier. He likewise figures importantly in the events described in the Epilogue.

The same season, when a local Lamichane boy was married, no Sora Jat clansmen attended his wedding. The following year when the son of the Ngor clansman, featured in the incident described, was married, a number of Char Jat men came at the express invitation of the boy's father. Most of those present were from the 'Seven House' lineages. They fully intended their attendance to be public knowledge, for already, within that year, the atmosphere of conflict had been changing. Later, in the spring of 1972, a Yoj wedding in lineage B was held to which several Lamichane and Ghale clansmen came by invitation. The gradual trend toward amelioration of the conflict began to grow.

The prohibition against performing labor and services was also interpreted at first to include the category of wage and cooperative group labor. In a major way it affected the organization and performance of nogar cooperative field work, and to a minor extent other small scale forms of cooperative labor exchange (*parma* and *guhar*). It has not greatly influenced most pre-existing individual wage and labor arrangements (*nimek*) except in one unique instance described below, and it has not affected the long-established system of share-cropping (*adhiya*) by which poorer villagers work the land of wealthier ones, of either jat, in return for half the harvest. The reason for its effect on nogar is because of that institution's intimate relationship to rodi. The reason for its minor effects on the other areas of cooperative work and share-cropping is primarily economic. Poorer Sora Jat villagers simply cannot afford to stop working for the wealthier Char Jat, despite their elders' admonitions to the contrary, and Char Jat landlord have no other ready source of laborers to work their fields. To disrupt this form of economic symbiosis would be extremely dysfunctional. Both parties have more to gain by maintaining as much economic stability as possible.

There is one instance of change in the patterns of individual wage labor. Few if any Sora Jat clansmen today would give serious consideration to working in any capacity for the council chairman and his half-brother, the Jimuwal of Lamichane lineage D. The reason is that these wealthy men have been very outspoken against the Sora Jat and have quite openly maintained an air of status superiority, especially since the bean field dispute of 1970. As a result, the Jimuwal has sponsored a Magar family to the village to work his fields and carry his loads. He has given these ethnic outsiders a small house in Besi adjacent to his own, where they live and work in total dependence on him and his lineage brothers. On occasion, when other Char Jat persons need load carriers, they employ these Magars. But this option, not available generally to the other Char Jat villagers, is certainly an exception to the pattern of maintaining traditional economic symbiosis between the jats, and is the only example of its kind in Ghaisu.

CHANGING LAYMAN-RITUALIST RELATIONSHIPS

The third rule of the Sora Jat elders prohibits Sora Jat shamans, under threat of heavy fine, from conducting any rituals for Char Jat laymen. The first test of this new ruling came when lightning struck and burned a Lamichane shepherd's hut. It is the custom in such an event to summon a shaman immediately to perform a purification rite 'to return the flames' (*mi le seb*). When the Lamichane herdsman received word that the shaman would not come, he turned to the village lamas for help. Prior to that time the village lamas' only ritual duties outside of their own private devotions, saying mantras (spells) for the sick, and purifying houses, were at Char Jat Pai where they performed as disciples subordinate to the lama gurus.

Not long after the lightning incident, a death occurred in Lamichane lineage A. Always in the past, the shamans had conducted the initial mortuary rites and burial, but now that was uncertain. The threat of fine and of corporate displeasure deterred the shamans, although they personally wished to perform the rituals as usual. Several Lamichane clan elders met to discuss the matter and the council chairman requested that the village lamas be asked to officiate instead. Thus, for a second time the lamas were brought in to perform a service heretofore rendered by shamans. The Pai, held a few months later, was also conducted exclusively by lamas. It was the first Char Jat Pai conducted without shamans, and the contractural traditions regarding shamans as well as the rule regarding breach of contract were ignored (see Legend 5).

Ever since that occasion, the practice has been for the village lamas to officiate at all Char Jat burials and to assist the outside lamas at Pai. The shamans became available only to their own Sora Jat brothers for whom they continued to perform all regular ritual services. No lamas are ever hired by the Sora Jat, except as the lama who is a Yoj clansman performs Buddhist rituals for his own immediate family. The position of that Yoj lama has, in itself, some interesting implications.

The Yoj lama's anomalous role as a Sora Jat clansman is not, as one might expect, sufficient reason for him to refrain from performing ritual services for the Char Jat. His father's brother, the Yoj clan chief, is the most outspoken critic of the Char Jat in the village. At first he sought to dissuade his nephew from studying Buddhism, but he did not succeed. It is well known that the young lama and his father do not agree with the Yoj chief's strong feelings nor with the direction his leadership of the jat was taking. There is, furthermore, a long-standing animosity between the Yoj lama's immediate family and the *khepre* shaman's, which does not allow them to rely on the shamans to officiate at family rites. This may have been an incentive for the young Yoj to study Buddhism in the first place.

The fact that the Yoj lama's father is one of the wealthiest villagers has been an asset, for he has not had to depend upon anyone else for economic assistance and he has had ample time to puruse his religious studies. The Char Jat clansmen who hire him do not express any ill feelings against him because of his birthright. Some, in fact, are pleased with that situation for it is interpreted as further dividing the Sora Jat camp. In general, the Char Jat are very respectful of the Yoj lama's skilled and confident display of knowledge of the Buddhist ritual; those of the 'Seven House' Lamichane lineages prefer to hire him over the Lamichane lama of lineage G.

Although both village lamas are mere novices, since 1970 they have been accorded greater and greater respect as relatively learned ritualists. Char Jat informants frequently pointed with pride to "our lamas who read books," reflecting a widespread feeling in Nepal that education generally enhances the prestige of those associated with it.

To the Char Jat, hiring a lama reinforces status. Furthermore, the lamas' use of books represents a certain infallibility. The oral traditions of the shamans can be easily lost, forgotten, or badly recited, they claim. Other of the lamas' paraphernalia, such as prayer flags, also add to their favor among the Char Jat. In contrast, the shamans and other Sora Jat clansmen point with as much pride to their oral traditions which, they contend, keep alive the ancient Gurung myths and rituals.

Changes in use of ritual specialists has further widened the breach between the jats, reinforcing boundaries across which normal priest-client and many other relationships are no longer tolerated. Sora Jat exclusiveness in prohibiting their shamans from serving the Char Jat gave them an initial advantage over the Char Jat and was a manipulative power play. In the long run it was self-defeating, for the Char Jat had a ready and acceptable alternative in the village lamas. The Char Jat clansmen have interpreted the change to lama ritualists as a step upward in ritual status, a further demonstration of their superiority vis-a-vis the Sora Jat. But the transition was not smooth. Allegations of status superiority were met with counter claims by the Sora Jat, and dissention also arose within the ranks of the Char Jat over certain ritual proscriptions imposed by the lamas. The more significant of these impositions occurred in funeral rites and feasts.

CHANGES IN FUNERARY CEREMONIES

Earlier, shamans and lamas were contrasted in the context of rituals of death. To recapitulate, there are four primary differences between them:

1. Their paraphernalia differ.

2. Lamas recite from books while shamans rely on oral tradition.

3. The lamas perform no dance or gestures resembling that called *o nob* where the shaman raises his feet over the corpse.

4. Lamas prohibit all forms of blood sacrifice.

The first two differences have already been discussed. The third and fourth items are important in a ritual sense and have been given by the Char Jat as two reasons why they no longer employ shamans. This is probably retrospective, for it has only been since employing lamas that the Char Jat have objected to the shamans in these terms. The raising of the Sora Jat shaman's feet over the corpse of a Char Jat clansman is now considered a ritually defiling gesture, one certainly not commensurate with alleged Char Jat status superiority. Much has been made of this concern for ritual purity and superiority in Ghaisu, and it is doubtful now that should a shaman agree to conduct a Char Jat funeral he would be allowed to perform that gesture or be given the deferential foot bathing which follows. In many respects, the foot bathing by the Char Jat and the act of *syo laba* at Ghanto, both focused on the Sora Jat, are related phenomena.

Finally, the lamas as Buddhists prohibit all forms of blood sacrifice, while for the shamans sacrifice is an integral and essential part of virtually all ritual. Since employing lamas, the Char Jat have openly condemned blood sacrifice at the insistence of the lamas, thereby negating an ancient Gurung tradition.

The prohibition of blood sacrifice by the lamas and the thought of a meatless final feast at Amel, however, has caused considerable concern among the Char Jat. The lamas justify their stance against sacrifice in terms of general Buddhist precepts about the sanctity of life, but they admittedly can find no direct reference to it in their books apropos of Pai. The problem is one of accommodating Buddhist ritual to Gurung tradition by the lamas and laymen alike. The laymen were willing to concede to Buddhist practice at first, assured that no harm would come if the prestigous lamas, whom they now hold in esteem above all ritualists, were in charge. Furthermore, the Char Jat are confident that monastic tradition imparts greater authority and efficacy to ritual however performed. All of these changes were interpreted as strengthening claims to social and ritual superiority by the employers of the lamas, a consideration which initially outweighed all others.

When it actually came to serving meatless feasts, however, the Char Jat laymen balked. Serving meat to guests, especially to the honored affines, is a point of honor among Gurungs and one is expected to return the gesture. Meat is particularly important at such public occasions as Pai and Amel. Since it is an expensive luxury, most Pai are postponed until they can be combined and expenses pooled in order to provide the necessary meat. In the past, when shamans directed their blood sacrifices adjacent to the lamas, there was always enough flesh to meet requirements. Now, without shamans, there is no occasion for ritual butchering. Furthermore, it bothered the Char Jat that Sora Jat were accusing the Char Jat of being miserly in avoiding the expense.

The controversy over sacrifice or non-sacrifice permeated every Char Jat Pai in Ghaisu during the period of study, yet, none were meatless. The Char Jat succeeded in obtaining the flesh by killing the animals out of sight of the lamas, against their wishes, and in a novel non-ritual context. The lamas subsequently joined in eating the meat, however, for consumption is not prohibited. But not until a Lamichane Pai in early 1972, for a young Gurkha soldier killed in Bangladesh, did the lamas condescend to allow non-religious butchering expressly for the final feast of Amel. They compromised by saying, in effect, that what they did not witness was none of their concern and out of their jurisdiction. In short, tradition prevailed, albeit in a modified sort of way.

In the inter-jat conflict, the concern for honoring affines is also relevant where those affines, particularly the wife-giving *asyo* are of the opposite jat due to a union across jat lines. While marrying out of jat is theoretically prohibited, it is not an uncommon occurence. In such an instance, the need for the *asyo* affines

130

and their requisite gifts conflicts with the desire to avoid further relations between the jats. The conflict of interests is usually resolved by requesting classificatory *asyo* of one's own jat to serve in place of the real *asyo* of the other jat. This conflict has only occurred in one such instance recently in Ghaisu, and that was several years prior to the current disruptive confrontation. At that time the widowed mother of the present council chairman of Lamichane lineage D died. She was a Sora Jat woman of the Yoj clan, and a Ghaisu villager by birth. When time came for her Lamichane son to commence Pai, her Yoj brothers, the true *asyo* of her husband, were not invited. Rather, his affines through a second wife, a Char Jat woman of the Ghodane clan, were summoned from a distant village.

Conflict Control and Reintegration

Victor Turner's fourth stage in the "social drama" of conflicts and crises is that of "reintegration or . . . recognition of irreparable breach" (*op. cit.*). This stage in the Ghaisu conflict is represented not so much as another processual development phase of crisis, but by recognition of cleavage as well as by attempts to control and reintegrate the society. One possible impression of this final phase in Ghaisu is that the conflict has resulted in an irreversible schism in normal associations and in the emphatic redefinition of values concerning status and hierarchy. From the perspective of the Char Jat, for example, status distinctions have been reaffirmed. Ritual superiority is all the more clearly articulated as lamas take the place of shamans. From the Sora Jat perspective, however, the whole concept of status has been redefined, ostensibly neutralizing some distinctions. A gross disparity in perception of ends is obvious at this point, and the results of the conflict so far have been to neither equalize status nor to integrate the jats, as the Sora Jat elders have sought initially. Rather, quite the opposite has occurred: boundaries between the jats have been all the more sharply defined with the Hindu model of caste hierarchy clearly delineated and jat distinctions ever more sharply drawn.

Traditional Gurung interaction relationships and boundaries have been shuffled a bit, and certain preconceived notions of superiority have been challenged, but ultimately, the dominant cleavage between the jats has been reaffirmed and strengthened in subtle but sure ways. The "recognition of irreparable breach" is essentially, for Ghaisu villagers, the recognition that jat identity and separateness still exist certainly along economic lines, and to varying degrees along social, political, religious and other cultural lines as well. In the long run, tradition reigns *almost* supreme, and has proven to be one of the most difficult barriers to change. In the Ghaisu situation, where the traditional bases of economic stability and symbiosis remain highly valued, such tradition may best be left untampered for the time being, while other avenues of change may be more successfully explored (such as in the political sphere, the locus of a related sort of power and status).

High value is placed on tradition in general, and the villagers recognize that some changes may bring no appreciable or valuable improvement to life. This has led some villagers to make distinctions between what are and are not legitimate interaction areas in which to puruse conflict strategies, and has led some as well to actively seek to "reintegrate" the village along older, more traditional lines. Compartmentalization is one way to keep the conflict within locally acceptable bounds, and Amelioration is perceived as a step toward the normalization of relationships again. Both Compartmentalization and Amelioration are now discussed as part of the normalization scheme emerging from the Ghaisu data.

COMPARTMENTALIZATION

> By classifying people into categories, by specifying what sets of categories (such as those of age, occupation, or class) are appropriate to what occasions, and by indicating the statuses that each of these categories has in relation to others, people endeavour to regulate conflicts among them resulting from their incompatible wants.
> [Goodenough 1963: 96].

The villagers of Ghaisu perceive certain compartments of interaction and categories of identity which are sacrosanct, off-limits to the conflict. Over time certain categories of economic activity were considered beyond the bounds of conflict. They have been discussed above, and the conclusions are that the breach of certain interpersonal work relationships - *adhiya* and *nimek* in particular - would be decidedly dysfunctional to the economic well being of all concerned.

H. G. Barnett, noted for his major study of innovative behavior, calls these types of differentiations of expression and action "rationalized distinctions" which function as "cultural preservatives" (1953: 400, 166). Such rationalizations are significant, he indicates, in part because they become charters for belief and action. Furthermore,

> Human beings are able to live with their contradictory behaviors because of the facility with which they are able to compartmentalize their thinking. When they are confronted with the fact of their conflicting attitudes towards the same thing, they manufacture some distinction ... [A] rationalized distinction is made possible by the critical value of context or association [1953: 400].

One important compartmentalization in Ghaisu occurs in the office of the Jimuwal in the status of his person, and in the status relationships which exist between him and villagers of both jats at the time of Dasai. On the day of blessing, household heads of both jats pay their respects, in the form of deferential behavior, to the Jimuwal, and he, in turn, bestows the King's blessing upon them. There, seemingly despite any personal enmity which exists toward the man, the *office of Jimuwal* is still highly regarded, compartmentalized off, as it were, from the conflict. It is clear that while deferential behavior in some spheres of inter-personal and social interaction (for example at Ghanto and between Char Jat laymen and the shamans) have been abrogated, others have been maintained as sacred, according to the public value placed on them.

One reason sometimes given for distinct differences in behavior from one realm to another is that persons, social identities, seldom act with singularity or uniformity in every aspect of social interaction. Each actor has many identities, and many statuses in life. The multi-dimensional nature of identity and status makes it difficult to maintain an identical stance in every interaction situation.

> Keep in mind that a spate of deferential behavior is not a single note expressing a single relationship between two individuals active in a single pair of capacities, but rather a medley of voices answering to the fact that actor and recipient are in many different relationships to one another, no one of which can usually be given exclusive and continuous determinancy of ceremonial conduct. [Goffman 1956: 480]

Hence, an identity relationship in one setting may not necessarily be apropos in some other, and not infrequently, one identity or an aspect of an identity takes precedence, allowing for deferential behavior without concern for other possible identities. Thus, in the example of the Jimuwal, regardless of feelings toward the person who occupies the role, dutiful compliance to the traditions of his office and to the occasion of the blessing of the King are in order. Compartmentalization allows conduct to be consistent in this setting while being seemingly inconsistent in the larger conflict situation.

AMELIORATION: AN EPILOGUE

Ghaisu society will probably never return to the status quo as it existed before the bean field controversy, the rodi incidents, the abrogation of fictive kin relationships, and all the other disruptive events of 1970 and following. Rather, the status conflict will likely continue on several levels, and its consequences met and accommodated to for some time to come. By the time my research in Ghaisu was ending, however, certain conciliatory gestures designed to reintegrate village society and to ameliorate the dispute were apparent. Some of the villagers hoped for and actively promoted an early return to stable, cooperative relationships between the jats; that is, between them and their friends and neighbors. They saw it as the only hope for maintaining economic and social stability.

Amelioration began taking place between certain lineages and clans and between specific individuals. Among others it may never occur in this generation. It is quite unlikely, for instance, that the old Yoj chief will ever become friends with the Lamichane council chairman and his half-brother. Elsewhere there are more encouraging signs. Members of the 'Seven House Lamichane' lineages are currently among the most active in seeking peace. They are led by the former village Mukhya who has always been a peacemaker. His motivations do not appear to be political or selfish, rather that he wishes to secure lasting harmony in his village before he dies. Most Char Jat clansmen respect and follow his lead. Many Sora Jat clansmen also seek peaceful and cooperative relations and accept his wise counsel. It is clear that none of them will ever again perform overtly servile or demeaning roles vis-a-vis the Char Jat, but economic conditions will force them to ignore some conflicts of interest and it is to be expected that individual wage and group cooperative labor for wealthier villagers of both jats will continue.

The relationships most easily restored between the jats are the *ngyel* fictive kinship ties and the cooperative labor and financial arrangements at the lineage and clan levels. The ban on shamans performing Char Jat rituals will likely be eased and the shaman guru may once again be employed for minor Char Jat rituals. Both parties have expressed this desired end.

In early 1972, the Nasi clan chief died. He was one of the most outspoken of all Sora Jat elders in the conflict, second only to the Yoj chief himself. This man is the one said to have decreed the rules against jat interaction and to have been a vociferous contender in occasional public confrontations with Char Jat leaders.

Two days prior to his death, as he lay ill in his house, he called a younger Nasi kinsman, his heir, to his side and said:

nga sim tyaregya, nga akha;
nga polu su;
nga yamo tyare, nasa sage tat.

[I am dying, I cannot go on;
My mouth has been like the nettles' sting;
I am going now and it is time that the village reunites.]

Word of this confession-cum-admonition spread quickly through the village. The elder who spoke it had always been a respected person. In life he had served as a Gurkha officer. He was also an astrologer, diviner, and healer, and a man of great prestige and dominance in the affairs of his clan, jat, and village. His words in life and those at death were considered important and to be listened to. Those at the end were spoken at a time when a number of persons were voicing increased discontent with continual confrontation and wished for change toward normalcy. They provided an impetus towards improving inter-jat relations.

The younger kinsman to whom he spoke was not his son (he had no son), but was, nonetheless, heir to the clan chiefdomship. He was the Nasi whose daughter had borne the child of a Lamichane boy, and he was also one of those men fined for attending a Char Jat wedding. On the death of the old Nasi chief, the younger man would inherit great responsibilities, including the responsibility for hosting the commemorative rites of the old man's Pai. The young Nasi's own sympathies were to restore good inter-jat relations and he made a point to invite the Char Jat to the Nasi chief's Pai and Amel in the Fall. Many came.

Notes

1. Char Jat prestige reflects, to a great degree, the power that wealth commands. It is also true that councilmen tend to be chosen from among the ex-Gurkha soldiers of the community, a trend noted elsewhere among the Gurungs (Pignede 1962: 118) and widespread in Nepal.
2. In Ghaisu, the fine for the man is usually double that of the woman, the opposite of that reported here by Macfarlane.
3. One term which some Sora Jat informants use to designate the category of servile labor is *gha karni*. As an idiom of Nepalese derivation, it means a category of low, base, or otherwise demeaning labor. It is used in a derisive sense and has overt sexual connotations.

Glossary

TERM(S) OR IDIOM	DERIVATION*	PAGE IN TEXT**	DEFINITION

*Derivation of each term: N=Nepali, G=Gurung, T=Tibetan, Th=Thakali, H=Hindi, and E=English.
**Page numbers indicate where the term or idiom is first defined in the text.

TERM(S) OR IDIOM	DERIVATION	PAGE	DEFINITION
adhiyā	[N]	p. 36	'halves,' sharecropping
alā̃	[G]	p. 86	funeral flag, shroud
amal	[N]	p. 17	office, position, honor, respect, greatness
amali, amaldar	[N]	p. 17	village official; person holding office of *amal*
amel	[N]	p. 101	feast day following funeral memorial; separation
arghun	[N]	p. 74ff	commemorative funeral rites (Pai)
āshīk	[N]	p. 47	blessing
astamī	[N]	p. 68	'eighth' day of the month; the second day of Dasai
āsyõ, āsyõ-mai (pl.)	[G]	p. 86	wife-giving affines
āsyõ kwẽ	[G]	p. 86	gift of cloth from the *āsyõ* affines
āsyõ ka chob	[G]	p. 100	the 'lid closing affines'
āsyõ kai	[G]	p. 99	gift of food from the *āsyõ* affines
āsyõ pa	[G]	p. 99	gift of drink (liquor) from the *āsyõ* affines
āsyõ-mai bichhyauna	[GN]	p. 101	seating the *āsyõ* affines on woollen blankets

āsyõ-mai phu laba	[G]	p. 101	to please the *āsyõ* affines
bāramāsyā ghāto	[NG]	p. 73	a type of Ghanto dance-drama requiring drums
barga, barkha	[G, N]	p. 65	Gurung-Tibetan astrologic cycle of 12 years.
bayu thhe	[NG]	p. 79	spirit worship
bhāi, bhāi-mai (pl.)	[N, NG]	p. 46	brother, brothers
bhāi ngi tho seba	[NGGG]	p. 112	a form of cooperative friendship between clans
bhater	[N]	p. 61	wedding banquet
biyā laba	[NG]	p. 57	wedding
bla-ma	[T]	p. 6	lama
blon	[T]	p. 21	high officer of state, minister, governor (see *plon*)
can (i.e. chan)	[N?]	p. 17	assistants to the Nepali king of Lamjung; progenitors of the Lamichane clan
chār bhāi	[N]	p. 11	'four brothers'; the Char Jat sub-tribe
chār jāt	[N]	p. 4ff.	'four clans'; one of the two sub-tribes of Gurung
chaubisi rājā	[N]	p. 16	'twenty-four kings' of West Nepal
che to-bai mhī	[G]	p. 100	'demon stabbing man'; an exorcism ritual during Pai
chha sukā chyob	[N]	p. 61	'to count six quarters' (Rs. 1.50); a gift to the bride's mother by the groom
chhyāl yab	[G]	p. 62	'to go make up'; a gesture of request for mercy from the son-in-law to the father of the girl he has eloped with
chiba	[G]	p. 18	clan chief
chinu	[N]	p. 79	personal symbol, token
chulo nimta	[N]	p. 61	'hearth invitation'; a small wedding feast

dāg bātti laba	[NNG]	p. 95	'to do the firebrand'; a ritual of placing the first coal in the mouth of the deceased at cremation
dāg bātti mor misa mrõ	[NNGGG]	p. 95	'firebrand moustache eyebrow field'; a gift of land given to the man who substitutes for the son of the deceased at *dāg bātti laba*
dān	[N]	p. 76	gift
dapthar	[N]	p. 69	clan ledger of ancestors' names
dasaĩ	[N]	p. 66	pan-Hindu religious festival honoring the goddess Durga
dāsi putra	[N]	p. 13	'servants' son'
dhāmi	[N]	p. 103	wizard, sorcerer
dharni	[N]	p. 84	dry measure, approximately five pounds
dhashami	[N]	p. 69	'tenth' day of the month, the fourth day of Dasai
ḍhikur	[Th]	p. 36	a type of rotating credit association
dhoti	[N]	p. 79	white lower garment worn by Brahman men
dudh pokharī	[N]	p. 52	'milk lake'; one of many high mountain lakes considered sacred and popular pilgrimage goal for Hindus
durgā ghar	[N]	p. 68	the building housing the image of the goddess Durga
durgā pujā	[N]	p. 66	worship of the goddess Durga at Dasai
gaj patra	[N]	p. 83	a contract between a patron and client
gaun pãchayat	[N]	p. 107	'village council' form of local government

ghā karni	[N]	p. 135	a category of servile labor with overt sexual connotations.
ghale	[N]	p. 5	a Char Jat clan of legendary kings
ghale rājā	[N]	p. 5	king of the Ghale clan, and king of all Gurungs in legendary accounts
ghaneri	[G]	p. 73	girls' working committee for Ghanto
ghãto	[G]	p. 71ff.	Gurung dance-drama performed each spring by the Sora Jat
ghodāne	[N]	p. 5	a Char Jat clan of legendary ministers to the Ghale kings
'go-gnas	[T]	p. 5	official position in Tibetan polity
'go-pa	[T]	p. 5	village headman in Tibetan polity
gotra	[N]	p. 10	a named exogamous patrilineal clan; particularly one of several Brahman clans of legendary origin
guhār	[N]	p. 36	a cooperative work system of help or assistance
gurung-ko vamsāvali	[N]	p. 9	the Gurung genealogy or legend of origins
hukkhā	[N]	p. 76	water pipe for smoking
jajaman	[N]	p. 83	the patron, benefactor, employer of a priest
jajamani	[N]	p. 83	the contractual institution involving a *jajaman* and a priest
jamĩndar (zamĩndār)	[N]	p. 20n	'dominant landlord' of southern Nepal and India
jamnār yāb	[N]	p. 57	'going with the gift of drink,' a gesture performed during marriage arrangements

janai, janae	[N]	p. 79	holy cord worn by the high 'twice born' castes
janti parseb	[NG]	p. 58	'to cleanse the wedding party,' a gesture performed by village elders as the wedding party enters the groom's house
jatrā	[N]	p. 52	festival
jatrā yāba	[NG]	p. 52	going to a festival
jhā̃kri	[N]	p. 103	Nepalese shaman or diviner
jhāure nāch	[N]	p. 76	popular song and dance in the Nepali style
jimuwāl	[N]	p. 6	local land tax collector
jokar	[E]	p. 82	joker or comic actor
jogi	[N]	p. 82	joker or comic actor, *jokar*
jogi laba	[NG]	p. 76	comic acting
juṭh laidib	[NG]	p. 96	to be possessed of the pollution of death
juṭho	[N]	p. 96	pollution, defilement
kājī	[N]	p. 124	a patron-client system of 'workers'
kalas	[N]	p. 11n	a copper pot used in Hindu weddings
kaṭ mar	[N]	p. 68	ritual blood sacrifice
khema	[G]	p. 98	ancestors
kheprẽ	[G]	p. 77	a class of Sora Jat shamans a Sora Jat clan
khet	[N]	p. 18n	irrigated land
khhrõ	[G]	p. 6	the Char Jat sub-tribe
		p. 6	the Lamichane clan
		p. 6	village headman or chief
kle	[G]	p. 5	the Ghale clan
khheu piba	[G]	p. 101	'great gift giving', the final feast of Amel officiated by lamas

khĩ chũb	[G]	p. 58	the final wedding rite whereby the bride eats her first meal at the hearth of her husband
khle	[G]	p. 98	master, lord, chief, king; a shaman's patron diety
kolo	[G]	p. 50	young, prepubescent girl
kon	[G]	p. 5	the Ghodane clan
korsĩ	[N]	p. 61	payment of compensation at wedding or elopement
kothi	[N]	p. 34	dwelling
kot pujā	[N]	p. 68	armory worship during Durga Puja
kra nõb	[G]	p. 96	'to darry the head', an honor bestowed upon the most prestigous of the deceased being memorialized at Pai
kramo	[G]	p. 48	gift to a woman, a shawl
kregī	[G]	p. 48	gift to a man, a white turban
kromchẽ	[G]	p. 9	a Sora Jat clan
ku-gi	[G]	p. 27	'nine clans'; the Sora Jat (locally in the Modi River Valley)
lama, lam	[N]	p. 6	Char Jat clan of Buddhist monks
lāmichhāne	[N]	p. 6	the Char Jat clan allegedly subordinate to the Lama, but locally powerful in Lamjung District (see *khhrõ*)
lanãs	[G]	p. 100	'village of god', heaven
lekhāli	[N]	p. 2	highland Gurungs
lem	[G]	p. 6	the Lamichane clan
maie-mai rodī	[G]	p. 49	boys' rodi
maya	[N]	p. 51	love, affection
mgon	[T]	p. 5	lord

mhĩ du kaĩ	[G]	p. 101	'men together rice'; the final feast of Amel officiated by a shaman
mhĩ sibari	[G]	p. 85	the disposal of the corpse by burial or cremation
mi le sĕb	[G]	p. 127	a ritual 'to return the flames' following lightning or fire
mit	[N]	p. 46ff.	fictive kinship bond brotherhood
mitini	[N]	p. 46	fictive bond sister
mit lagaunu	[N]	p. 46	to take a bond brother
mo, mo-mai (pl.)	[G]	p. 86	wife-receiving affine, or son-in-law
mrĩ	[G]	p. 95	sorrow
mrĩ nŏb	[G]	p. 96	'carrying sorrow,' mourning
mukyhā	[N]	p. 6, 18n	village headman
		p. 18	a type of land revenue collector
myar dhurab	[G]	p. 100	'turn by turn performing'; a ritual gesture to provide the deceased the tools and materials necessary for afterlife.
nāchari	[N]	p. 102	dance
nāmi	[G]	p. 79	the shaman's ritual bird
narĩ maie-mai	[G]	p. 52	'guide boys' who chaperone rodi girls on pilgrimage
nãsi	[G]	p. 9	A Sora Jat clan
naumi	[N]	p. 68	'ninth' day of the month; third day of Dasai
neb	[G]	p. 83	host, patron
nge	[G]	p. 86	matrilineage
ngebār	[G]	p. 57	mediator in wedding arrangements
ngor	[G]	p. 9	A Sora Jat clan

ngorsyo-phlesyo bayu	[GGN]	p. 80	spirit worship honoring deceased girls of the Ngor and Phle clans
ngyel, ngyela, ngyeloh	[G]	p. 46ff.	fictive kinship, bond brother
ngyel bhai-mai	[GNG]	p. 46	fictive brothers
ngyel chyab	[G]	p. 46	to take a bond brother
ngyelsyo	[G]	p. 46	fictive bond sister
ngyel su	[G]	p. 48	'mouth bond'; so-called fictive kinship
nimek	[N]	p. 36	individual wage labor
nõ	[G]	p. 58	general reciprocity
nõgar	[G]	p. 51	cooperative work party organized by rodi
nõgar syo kaĩ	[G]	p. 52	a feast for the nogar work party
õ nõb	[G]	p. 95	ritual gesture of expelling demons performed by shaman over the corpse
pãcha khat	[N]	p. 18n	a class of crimes referred to government courts
pai	[G]	p. 96ff.	final memorial rites for the dead
paĩ	[G]	p. 6	a western Gurung term for lamichane clan
paĩcho	[G]	p. 86	a form of lending help among clans
paĩdi	[G]	p. 80	astrologer
pajyu	[G]	p. 77	a class of Sora Jat shamans
		p. 9	A Sora Jat clan
pakho	[N]	p. 18n	unirrigated land
pālik	[G]	p. 61	social reciprocity
pālik cheb	[G]	p. 61	a social debt outstanding
paraphrẽ	[G]	p. 73	boys' working committee for Ghanto

parma	[N]	p. 36	a cooperative system of mutual labor exchange
pāte bhāi-mai	[N? NG]	p. 112	institution of cooperative friendship between clans
phaili thhe	[G]	p. 69	ancestor worship
phale khrub	[G]	p. 58	'foot bathing'; washing the bride's feet before marriage
phale khrub mwi	[G]	p. 58	money given in conjunction with *phale khrub*
phi krodzeb	[G]	p. 96	announcement of the dates for Pai
phle	[G]	p. 9	a Sora Jat clan
phreje-rhejer prabai mhī	[G]	p. 97	the man who goes to summon guests to Pai
phre kaĩ	[G]	p. 50	'separation meal' served to the bride by rodi girls on the eve of her wedding
phrẽsyo rhīnab	[G]	p. 57	bethrothal
phurba	[T]	p. 82	ritual dagger
phūl pāti	[N]	p. 68	'flowers and leaves' used to decorate the image of Durga during Dasai
phwolī wab	[G]	p. 58	wedding ritual to dispell hostilities between families
pla	[G]	p. 98	effigy of the dead
plih-gi	[G]	p. 21	'four clans'; the Char Jat (among western Gurungs)
plon	[G]	p. 6	The Lamichane clan (among western Gurungs); see *blon*
pradhān pãch	[N]	p. 107	Panchayat assembly chairman
pujāri	[N]	p. 69	priest, priestly attendant to a deity
purohit	[N]	p. 12	personal priest
pwaeme	[G]	p. 21	'Tibetan'; a Sora Jat sub-tribe (among western Gurungs)

pyõgu	[G]	p. 79	small pottery jug, token of the *kheprẽ* shaman guru of Ghaisu
rāj putra	[N]	p. 13	'royal son'; a king's son
rājā ko tikā	[N]	p. 69	the King's blessing
raksi	[N]	p. 57	liquor
rhi	[G]	p. 98	'bone'?; bone dust used in Pai ceremony
rĩ chame	[G]	p. 96	sisters, daughters, and wives together; one's female relatives
rĩ-mai rodī	[G]	p. 49	girls' dodi
roba	[G]	p. 64	to sleep
rodī	[G]	p. 49ff.	Gurung youth association
rodī āb, ro āb	[G]	p. 50	rodi father, sponsor
rodī ām	[G]	p. 50	rodi mother sponsor
rodī ghar	[GN]	p. 49	rodi house
rodī laba	[G]	p. 49	'to do rodi' (i.e. to take part in rodi)
rodī tĩ	[G]	p. 49	rodi house
rodir-bai rĩ-mai	[G]	p. 50	girl friends or members in rodi
romai	[G]	p. 61	gift
sabhā	[N]	p. 107	assembly, council
saĩdi ghãto	[G]	p. 73	a type of Ghanto dance-drama requiring no drum accompaniment
samsyo	[G]	p. 50	bride's maid
sat ghare	[N]	p. 31	'seven house'; a Lamichane lineage of Ghaisu
serga kwe	[G]	p. 101	funeral dance and song
shiso	[G]	p. 77	disciple to a guru
so	[G]	p. 98	breath of life
sora bhāi	[N]	p. 11	'sixteen brothers'; the Sora Jat

sora jāt	[N]	p. 4ff.	'sixteen clans'; one of the two sub-tribes of Gurungs
subbā	[N]	p. 27n	official appointee with customs revenue collection and certain magistrate's duties
syo laba	[G]	p. 114	gesture of obeisance toward an elder
tamu	[G]	p. 77n	Gurung term for themselves
te nõ teb	[G]	p. 58	wedding rite formalizing the alliance between two families or lineages
ṭetar	[E]	p. 52	'theatre'; youthful song, dance, and comedy acts.
ṭetar laba	[EG]	p. 52	'to do theatre'
thā, thā-mai (pl.)	[G]	p. 4n	primary patrilineal descent group; men of the local lineage
theba	[G]	p. 50	a teenage, or pubescent, girl
tho seba	[G]	p. 68	ritual blood sacrifice
thokne	[N]	p. 73	boys who lead the working committees of Ghanto
thorchẽ	[G]	p. 9	A Sora Jat clan
tika	[N]	p. 71	a mark on the forehead (usually of rice or coloured powder)
		p. 47	a blessing
		p. 71	the fourth day of Dasai when the King's blessing is bestowed on the people
timur	[N]	p. 84	a popular aromatic spice and tonic (*Zanthoxylum armatum*)
trishul	[N]	p. 12	a trident used as a Hindu religious symbol
tu	[G]	p. 9	a Sora Jat clan
tũ pai	[G]	p. 97	combined funeral memorial (Pai) honoring two or more persons

Bibliography

ALLEN, N. J.
1968 *Some Problems in the Ethnography of the Peoples of Nepal and their Neighbors.* B. Litt. Thesis, Oxford University.
1973 Fourfold Classifications of Society in the Himalaya. IXth International Congress of Anthropological and Ethnological Sciences, Chicago. *(Forthcoming in* James Fisher, editor, *World Anthropology: The Himalayan Interface.* The Hague. Mouton.)

ANDORS, Ellen
1974 The Rodighar and its Role in Gurung Society. *Contributions to Nepalese Studies - Journal of the Institute of Nepal and Asian Studies, Tribhuvan University, Nepal* 1: 2: 10-24.
n.d. *The Life-cycle of Gurung Women: Child-Rearing Practices and Later Socialization in a Gurung Village.* Ph. D. Dissertation, Columbia University. (Forthcoming).

BARNETT, H. G.
1953 *Innovation: The Basis of Cultural Change.* New York: McGraw-Hill.

BISTA, Dor Bahadur
1967 *People of Nepal.* Kathmandu: Department of Publicity, His Majesty's Government.

BUCHANAN (HAMILTON), Francis
1819 *An Account of the Kingdom of Nepal and of the Territories Annexed to the Dominion by the House of Gorkha.* New Delhi. Manjusri, Bibliotheca Himalayica reprint, 1971.

CAPLAN, Lionel
1970 *Land and Social Change in East Nepal: A Study of Hindu-Tribal Relations.* Berkeley: University of California Press.

CARRASCO, Pedro
1959 *Land and Polity in Tibet.* Seattle: University of Washington Press.

COSER, Lewis
1956 *The Functions of Social Conflict.* New York: Free Press.

DOHERTY, Victor
1974 The Organizing Principles of Gurung Kinship. *Kailash - A Journal of Himalayan Studies* 3: 4: 273ff.
1975 *Kinship and Economic Choice: Modern Adaptations in West Central Nepal.* Ph.D. Dissertation, University of Wisconsin, Madison.

DUMONT, Louis
1970 *Homo Hierarchicus: An Essay on the Caste System,* translated by Mark Sainsbury. Chicago: University of Chicago Press.

ELIADE, Mircea
1964 Shamanism : Archaic Techniques of Ecstasy, Princeton, N.J: Princeton University Press.

ELWIN, Verrier
1947 *The Muria and their Ghotul.* Bombay: Oxford University Press.
1968 *The Kingdom of the Young.* Bombay: Oxford University Press.

FISHER, James F.
1973 Homo Hierarchicus Nepalensis, a Cultural Sub-species. IXth International Congress of Anthropological and Ethnological Sciences, Chicago. (*Forthcoming in* James Fisher, editor, *World Anthropology: The Himalayan Interface.* The Hague: Mouton.)

FÜRER-HAIMENDORF, Christoph von
1938 The Morung System of the Konyak Nagas, Assam. *Journal of the Royal Anthropological Institute* 68: 349-378.
1960 Caste in the Multi-Ethnic Society of Nepal. *Contributions to Indian Sociology* 4: 12-32.
1968 *The Konyak Nagas: An Indian Frontier Tribe.* New York: Holt, Rinehart and Winston.
1974 The Changing Fortunes of Nepal's High Altitude Dwellers, *in* Christoph von Fürer-Haimendorf, editor, *Contributions to the Anthropology of Nepal* (Proceedings of a Symposium held at the School of Oriental and African Studies, University of London, June/July 1973.) Warminster, England: Aris & Phillips, Ltd. Pp. 98-113.
1975 *Himalayan Traders.* New York : St. Martin's Press.

GHURYE, G. S.
1950 *Caste and Class in India.* Bombay: Popular Book Depot.

GLOVER, Warren W.
1969 *Gurung Phonemic Summary* (Tibeto-Burman Phonemic Summaries, 1.) Kathmandu: Summer Institute of Linguistics, Tribhuvan University. (Mimeo)
1971 *A Devanagari Spelling System for the Gurung Language.* Kathmandu: Summer Institute of Linguistics, Tribhuvan University. (Mimeo)
1972 *A Vocabulary of the Gurung Language.* Kathmandu: Summer Institute of Linguistics, Tribhuvan University. (Mimeo)
1974 *Sememic and Grammatical Structures in Gurung (Nepal).* Kathmandu: Tribhuvan University Press for the Summer Institute of Linguistics of the University of Oklahoma.

GLOVER, Warren W. and Jessie R. GLOVER
1972 *A Guide to Gurung Tone.* (Guide to Tone in Nepal, 6). Kathmandu: Summer Institute of Linguistics, Tribhuvan University. (Mimeo)

GOFFMAN, Erving
1956 The Nature of Deference and Demeanor. *American Anthropologist* 58: 3: 473-502.

GOODENOUGH, Ward Hunt
1963 *Cooperation in Change.* New York: Russell Sage Foundation.
1965 Rethinking 'Status' and 'Role': Toward a General Model of the Cultural Organization of Social Relationships, *in* M. Banton, editor *The Relevance of Models for Social Anthropology.* London: Tavistock. Pp. 1-24.

HARI, Anna Maria (editor)
1971 *Conversational Nepali.* Kathmandu: Summer Institute of Linguistics, Tribhuvan University.

HASRAT, Bikrama Jit
1970 *History of Nepal, as Told by Its Own and Contemporary Chroniclers.* Krishan Nagar, Hoshiarpur, Punjab, India: B. J. Hasrat.

HITCHCOCK, John T.
1966 *The Magars of Banyan Hill.* New York: Holt, Rinehart and Wineston.
n.d. Ecologically Related Differences between a Transhumant and a Sedentary Himalayan Village. (Paper presented to a Symposium on Cultural Adaptation to Mountain Eco-Systems, American Anthropological Association Meetings, New Orleans 1973. Manuscript)

HODGSON, Brian H.
n.d. Miscellaneous notes on the Gurungs of Nepal, Volume 5, pp. 9-12, 44-45, and 75-78. London: India Office Library and Records. (Handwritten and unpublished)
1884 *Essays on the Languages, Literature and Religion of Nepal and Tibet Together with Further Papers on the Geography, Ethnology and Commerce of Those Countries.* Varanasi: Bharat-Bharati reprint, 1971.

JÄSCHKE, H. D.
1881 *A Tibetan-English Dictionary with Special Reference to the Prevailing Dialects to which is Added an English-Tibetan Vocabulary.* London: Routledge and Kegan Paul reprint, 1972.

MACFARLANE, Alan D. J.
1972 *Population and Economy in Central Nepal: A Study of the Gurungs.* Ph.D. Dissertation, University of London. *(Forthcoming as Resources and Population: A Study of the Gurungs of Nepal.* Cambridge, England: Cambridge University Press.)

MESSERSCHMIDT, Donald A.
1972 Rotating Credit in Gurung Society: The *Dhikur* Associations of Tingaun (Nepal). *The Himalayan Review* (Nepal Geographical Society, Kathmandu) 5: 4: 23-35.
1973 *Dhikur:* Rotating Credit Associations in Nepal. IXth International Congress of Anthropological and Ethnological Sciences, Chicago. (*Forthcoming in* James Fisher, editor *World Anthropology: The Himalayan Interface.* The Hague: Mouton.)
1974a Gurung Shepherds of Lamjung Himal. *Objets et Mondes* 14 : 4: 307-316.
1974b *Social Status, Conflict, and Change in a Gurung Community of Nepal.* Ph.D. Dissertation, University of Oregon, Eugene.
1975a Ethnographic Observations of Gurung Shamanism in Lamjung District, *in* John T. Hitchcock and Rex L. Jones, editors, *Spirit Possession in the Nepal Himalayas.* Warminster, England: Aris & Phillips, Ltd. pp. 197-216
1975b Gurung Shepherds of Lamjung Himal. *Objects et Mondes*, 14:4: 307-318.
n.d. Ecological Change and Adaptation among the Gurungs of the Nepal Himalaya. *Human Ecology* (forthcoming).

MESSERSCHMIDT, Donald A. and Nareshwar Jang GURUNG
1974 Parallel Trade and Innovation in Central Nepal: The Cases of the Gurung and Thakali Subhas Compared, *in* Christoph von Fürer-Haimendorf, editor, *Contributions to the Anthropology of Nepal* (Proceedings of a Symposium held at the School of Oriental and African Studies, University of London, June/July 1973.) Warminster, England: Aris & Phillips, Ltd. Pp. 197-221.

NEPAL, His Majesty's Government of
1962 *Village Panchayat Act, 1962 (Gaun Panchayat Ain, 2018), Amended, in* Nepal Law Translation Series 1/71 (1971): 1-51. Kathmandu: Nepal Press Digest (Pvt.), Ltd.
1973 1971 Population Census of Nepal. Kathmandu: HMG, National Planning Commission Secretariat, Central Bureau of Statistics.

OKADA, Ferdinand E.
1957 Ritual Brotherhood: A Cohesive Factor in Nepalese Society. *Southwestern Journal of Anthropology* 13: 212-222.

PIGNEDE, Bernard
1962 Clan Organization and Hierarchy among the Gurungs, *Contributions to Indian Sociology* 6: 102-119.
1966 *Les Gurungs: une Population Himalayenne du Nepal.* Paris: Mouton.

REGMI, Mahesh C.
1963 *The State as Landlord: Raikar Tenure.* (Land Tenure and Taxation in Nepal, 1). Institute of International Studies Research Series No. 3. Berkeley: University of California Press.
1971 *A Study in Nepali Economic History, 1786-1846.* New Delhi: Manjusri.

ROSE, Leo E. and Margaret W. FISHER
1970 *The Politics of Nepal: Persistence and Change in an Asian Monarchy.* Ithaca: Cornell University Press.

SHARMA, Bal Chandra
1962 *Nepali Shabda-kosh* (Nepali Dictionary). Kathmandu: Royal Nepal Academy.

SNELLGROVE, David L.
1967 *Four Lamas of Dolpo.* (Tibetan Biographies, 1; Introduction and Translations) Oxford: Bruno Cassirer.

SRIVASTAVA, Ram P.
1953 'Rang-Bang' in the Changing Bhotia Life. *Eastern Anthropologist* 6: 190-203.

STILLER, Ludwig F., S. J.
1973 *The Rise of the House of Gorkha: A Study in the Unification of Nepal, 1768-1816.* New Delhi: Manjusri.

TILMAN, H. W.
1952 *Nepal Himalaya.* Cambridge, England: Cambridge University Press.

TURNER, Ralph
1965 *A Comparative and Etymological Dictionary of the Nepali Language.* London: Routledge and Kegan Paul (revised from 1931 edition).

TURNER, Victor
1957 *Schism and Continuity in an African Society: A Study of Ndembu Village Life.* Manchester: Manchester University Press.

VANSITTART, E.
1916 *Gurkhas* (Handbook for the Indian Army). Calcutta: Superintendent of Government Printing (revised from 1906 edition).